M000027701

SI No.

GET HALA PAY AS YOU TALK TODAY

Pay QR25 and get QR25 credit!*

VOUCHER
QR25

Present this voucher worth QR25 together with your passport
or QID copy when you purchase a HALA Pay As You Talk SIM
at participating Qtel shops at Villaggio, Landmark or Al Wakra.
Pay ONLY QR25 and enjoy QR25 worth of free talk time.

* Offer is valid until 31st December 2009. This voucher may be
used only once.

www.qtel.com.qa

قطر
Qtel

Let's Connect

HALA

PAY AS YOU TALK

NO CONTRACT

UP TO 360 DAYS VALIDITY

OFF-PEAK RATES

BONUS CREDIT FOR
QR50 TOP-UPS AND HIGHER!

Qatar

Mini **Visitors'** Guide

Qatar Mini **Visitors'** Guide
ISBN – 978-9948-8588-0-5

Copyright © Explorer Group Ltd 2009
All rights reserved.

All maps © Explorer Group Ltd 2009

Front cover photograph: The Pearl Monument – Victor Romero

Printed and bound by
Emirates Printing Press, Dubai, UAE

Explorer Publishing & Distribution
PO Box 34275, Dubai, United Arab Emirates
Phone (+971 4) 340 8805 Fax (+971 4) 340 8806
info@explorerpublishing.com
www.live**work**explore.com

Introduction

Welcome to the *Qatar Mini Visitors' Guide*. This mini marvel, perfect for visitors, was prepared by the same team that brought you the *Qatar Explorer*. Written entirely by residents, you'll find all you need to make the most out of your time in this interesting country – whether it is the top restaurants, the most stylish shops or the best cultural spots. If you want to know more about Explorer Publishing, or tell us anything that we've missed, go to www.liveworkexplore.com.

Qatar Mini **Visitors'** Guide

Editorial Team: Pamela Afram, Jake Marsico, Ingrid Cupido
Authors: Fiona Murray, Mike Crosby, Mohanalakshmi Phongsavan, Rachel Morris, Skylar Sherman, Sue Page
Designer: Shawn Jackson Zuzarte
Photographers: Victor Romero, Pete Maloney, Pamela Grist, David Quinn, Jake Marsico
Proofreader: Jo Holden-MacDonald

Contents

2 Essentials
4 Marhaba!
6 Qatar Checklist
16 Best Of Qatar
18 Visiting Qatar
22 Local Knowledge
30 Media & Further Reading
32 Public Holidays & Annual Events
38 Getting Around
44 Places To Stay

50 Exploring
52 Explore Qatar
54 Al Sadd & Al Rayyan Road
58 Diplomatic Area & West Bay
64 Doha Corniche
70 Khalifa Street & Al Luqta Street
74 Salwa Road & Al Aziziyah
80 Souk Area & Souk Waqif
86 Outside Of Doha
92 Tours & Sightseeing

96 Sports & Spas
98 Active Qatar
112 Spectator Sports
120 Spas

122 Shopping
124 Shopping In Qatar
126 Hotspots
128 Markets & Souks
134 Shopping Malls
138 Department Stores
140 Where To Go For...

144 Going Out
146 Doha Delights
150 Venue Directory
154 Al Sadd & Al Rayyan Road
162 Diplomatic Area & West Bay
172 Doha Corniche
176 Khalifa Street & Al Luqta Street
178 Salwa Road & Al Aziziyah
192 Souk Area & Souk Waqif
202 Entertainment

206 Profile
208 Culture
214 History
220 Qatar Today

226 Maps

240 Index

Essentials

4 Marhaba!

6 Qatar Checklist

16 Best Of Qatar

18 Visiting Qatar

22 Local Knowledge

30 Media & Further Reading

32 Public Holidays & Annual Events

38 Getting Around

44 Places To Stay

FANAR

Marhaba!

Welcome to Qatar, a country of contrasts; high-rise buildings meet with authentic souks and modernity mixes with an enduring sense of tradition.

Qatar's current growth, ambitious developments and low crime rate have made it an attractive destination for a broad mix of international visitors. If you are touching down in this fascinating region for business or for pleasure, Qatar has a lot to offer. With year-round sunshine, golden beaches, outdoor activities and a fascinating culture and history, this is a prime tourist destination that remains relatively undiscovered.

Qatar doesn't necessarily want to attract mass tourism, but aims to become known as a high-quality destination that appeals to high-income sectors such as the Mice market (meetings, incentives, conferences and exhibitions).

To help achieve this the government is investing a massive $15 billion to develop Qatar's infrastructure. While most of the major international hotel chains are already represented in Qatar, investment will see a host of new hotels and resorts emerge to cater for the anticipated growth in visitor numbers. By summer 2010, Qatar will have an estimated 10,000 hotel rooms. As well as stand-alone hotels, there are a number of projects currently under way that will include facilities for tourists, such as Entertainment City, and The Pearl Qatar (p.60).

The majority of Qatar's population resides in the capital city, Doha. Other major towns in the country include Mesaieed, Dukhan, Al Khor, Al Shamal and Al Wakrah. Doha's

Doha skyline

mix of high rise buildings, traditional and contemporary architecture brings with it a variety of experiences for visitors, whether it is a picturesque stroll around the Corniche (p.7) or a spot of retail therapy at its comprehensive shopping malls (p.135) and souks (p.128). Culture vultures will find solace in its art galleries (p.52) and forts, while thrill seekers can venture outside of the city and participate in dune bashing and off-roading tours out towards the Inland Sea (p.90).

The following pages will help you familiarise yourself with Qatar. The Profile chapter (p.206) provides you with a solid background on Qatar's culture, tradition and people. The best spots to meet and eat are listed in Going Out (p.144), and you can find the best places to unwind or release some tension in the Sports & Spas chapter (p.96). Discover Qatar's rich heritage, from Doha Corniche (p.64) to Souq Waqif (p.80), in the Exploring chapter (p.50).

Qatar Checklist

01 Shop In Style

Modern malls such as Villaggio (p.135), City Center Doha (p.134) and Landmark (p.134) give shoppers plenty of opportunities to part with their hard-earned cash. And when you've shopped till you're ready to drop, there's no end of cafes, restaurants and cinemas to help revive the weary.

02 Conquer The Corniche

Perhaps the most picturesque part of the capital, the Corniche extends seven kilometres in a horseshoe around Doha Bay. The area is a popular destination for walkers and joggers who take the opportunity to exercise outdoors, but there are plenty of places to sit back and enjoy the skyline or the night lights. See p.64.

03 Step Back In Time

For a fascinating view of Qatar's history, escape from the city and travel north from Doha to Umm Salal Mohammed (p.90). You'll marvel at the ancient buildings and architecture, including the impressive fort and Barzan Tower.

04 Snap Up Fresh Fish

A visit to the fish market (p.76) is a great experience, especially if you can drag yourself out of bed before sunrise to watch the auctioning take place before the actual market opens to the public. Beware though, it is a bit of a smelly way to spend a morning.

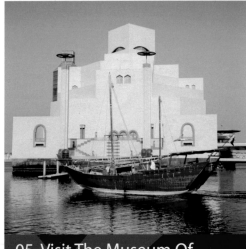

05 Visit The Museum Of Islamic Art

Set on the Corniche, this beautiful building designed by architect IM Pei is impressive. The museum was opened to the public in December 2008; it is an eagerly awaited boost to Doha's cultural offerings. See p.64.

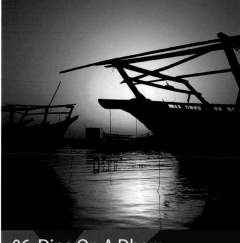

06 Dine On A Dhow

This is a fabulous way to see Doha from the water. The best time to take the cruise is in the evening, so you can enjoy the sunset and witness the city's skyline by night. Evening cruises will often include dinner and drinks too. See p.101.

07 Go Dune Bashing

Khor Al Adaid, also known as the 'Inland Sea' (p.90), is
at the south-eastern end of the country and requires
a four-wheel drive and an experienced driver to reach.
The towering dunes make it perfect for sand skiing or
boarding and its calm waters are great for swimming.

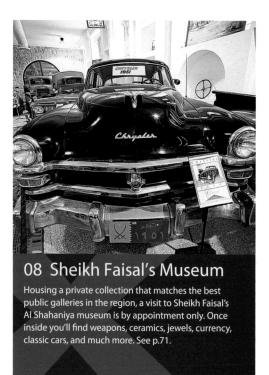

08 Sheikh Faisal's Museum

Housing a private collection that matches the best public galleries in the region, a visit to Sheikh Faisal's Al Shahaniya museum is by appointment only. Once inside you'll find weapons, ceramics, jewels, currency, classic cars, and much more. See p.71.

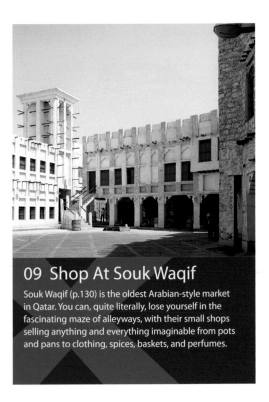

09 Shop At Souk Waqif

Souk Waqif (p.130) is the oldest Arabian-style market
in Qatar. You can, quite literally, lose yourself in the
fascinating maze of alleyways, with their small shops
selling anything and everything imaginable from pots
and pans to clothing, spices, baskets, and perfumes.

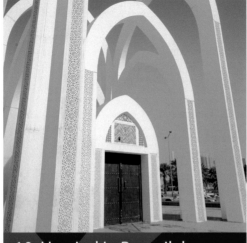

10 Unwind In Rumeilah Park

Sometimes referred to by its old name, Al Bidda, this public park opposite the Corniche is popular in the evening and at weekends. It has lots of green space, cafes and facilities, and a heritage village. See p.66.

For Adrenaline Junkies

The surrounding desert provides a great deal of interest for those looking for a bit of adventure. A trip to the 'Inland Sea', which is also known as Khor Al Adaid, (p.90) is a perfect excuse to get the adrenaline pumping, with a little help from a 4WD. As well as enjoying a bit of off-roading (p.94), dune bashing, and sand boarding (p.108), you can experience the areas wildlife. It is important to venture out with an experienced driver. There are a few tour companies (p.94) that offer off-roading trips out into the desert which often include a night camping out amongst the dunes.

For Big Spenders

Qatar's vast malls, plush hotels and spas offer no shortage of ways to spend some riyals. Begin your spree by staying at one of Doha's plush hotels offering a luxurious combination of palatial grounds, superior eateries and stylish bars. Then trot down to one of Doha's wide-ranging malls such as City Center Doha (p.134) or Villaggio (p.135) which offer a mix of high street brands, designer labels and electronics – and plenty to entertain kids while you satisfy your need for retail therapy. End the day with a bit of pampering at one of Doha's health spas (p.120). The Spa at the Marriott Doha (p.48) features Turkish baths to relax in, while the Six Senses Spa at Sharq Village & Spa (p.121) offers 23 treatment rooms and a plunge pool.

For Culture Buffs

There are a few points of interest for those looking for a touch of culture in Qatar. The Waqif Arts Center is located in Souk Waqif (p.130) and it houses some small galleries and shops. The Third Line Gallery (p.82), which also has a gallery in Dubai, can also be found here. The Orientalist Museum (p.82) displays work by artists like Eugene Dalacroix and Jose Villegas, while the eagerly anticipated Museum of Islamic Art (p.64), which has recently opened in Doha, features a broad variety of art on different mediums. The museum's three floors hold a vast selection of art originating from three continents, spanning from the seventh century to the present day. A few forts (p.87) and heritage sites (p.52) are dotted around Qatar, often in sparsely populated areas but many of them are under renovation.

For Water Babies

The region's warm water and golden beaches are the perfect environment for adrenaline seekers to enjoy watersports (p.104). Wakeboarding (p.110) and waterskiing (p.111) are popular here alongside parasailing (p.106) and diving (p.102). There is also a keen interest in powerboat racing (p.107). There are several sailing clubs in Qatar and events and regattas are held frequently. The Sealine Beach Resort (p.104) and the Diplomatic Club (p.106) both offer a good range of waterports.

Visiting Qatar

Qatar is a welcoming country which places few restrictions on its guests. Visitors will be charmed by the genuine warmth of the local people.

Getting There

Doha International Airport accommodates more than 20 passenger airlines and underwent an expansion programme to cater to the growing number of visitors to Qatar.

With Doha as its hub, the national carrier, Qatar Airways, has been expanding rapidly in recent years and now serves 82 destinations worldwide. The airline should start operating four Airbus A380 'superjumbos' by 2012. A new airport is being constructed a few kilometres away, ready to offer state of the art facilities to airlines and passengers. The new airport was designed specifically for the new superjumbos and will join Dubai International Airport as a major hub in long-haul flights to and from Asia and the west.

From The Airport

Most of the five-star hotels in Doha offer some variation of a return bus service for the airport. Arrival bus pickups are not currently in use. The available services do change on a regular basis but they are free and quite flexible. The best advice is to contact the concierge to verify the schedule or to request a drop-off for your specific flight. Doha International Airport offers a meet and greet service called Al Maha. Visit www. dohaairport.com for more information.

Airlines

Air France	432 1208	www.airfrance.com
Air India	432 4111	www.airindia.in
Biman Bangladesh	441 3422	www.bimanair.com
British Airways	432 1434	www.ba.com
Cyprus Airways	441 8666	www.cyprusairways.com
Delta Airlines	483 0725	www.delta.com
Egypt Air	445 8458	www.egyptair.com.eg
Emirates	438 4477	www.emirates.com
Gulf Air	445 5444	www.gulfairco.com
KLM	432 1210	www.klm.com
Kuwait Airways	443 5340	www.kuwait-airways.com
Pakistan International Air	442 6290	www.piac.com.pk
Qatar Airways	462 1717	www.qatarairways.com
Royal Jordanian	435 1422	www.rja.com.jo
Saudi Arabian Airlines	432 2991	www.saudiairlines.com
SriLankan Airlines	444 1217	www.srilankan.aero

Visas & Customs

For those planning short stays (under 21 days), a visit visa is perhaps the best option. Nationals of Gulf Cooperation Council (GCC) countries may enter Qatar without a visa, but all other nationalities require a visit visa. Residents of certain non-GCC countries are able to get a visit visa upon arrival, but others need to obtain the visa before travelling. This information is subject to change, so check with the Qatar Embassy or at www.moi.gov.qa before you fly. An immigration officer will stamp a 21 day visa into your passport on arrival. The visa will cost QR 100, but only credit or debit cards with Visa or MasterCard logos are accepted. This visa may later be extended for a month for QR 100. There are fines of QR 200 for each day that a visa is overstayed. Nationalities who are not eligible for a visa on arrival have several options: a sponsor based in Doha can apply for a visit visa, which are issued at the Immigration Department (airport section), or most of the major hotels can arrange tourist visas (sometimes at quite short notice) at a cost of QR 250, as well as a variable service charge. It's wise to enquire about the procedure when making a hotel reservation. These visas are for two weeks and can be extended by two weeks for QR 200.

For those travelling to Qatar on business, visas can be obtained by the partner company which is sponsoring your visit, or by a recognised government establishment such as a ministry. Business visas are valid for between 14 days and three months. Hotels can also arrange business visas (valid for three months at a cost of approximately QR 1,200). Again, check with the hotel prior to travelling.

Visitor Information In Qatar

Qatar's tourism sector is only just taking off. As yet, there are no government sponsored tourism offices. Visitors can check www.experienceqatar.com or www.qatar-tourism.com for basic travel information. One of the best web resources for travel information is the government's English web portal. To access, type 'Qatar Hukoomi' into your search engine. Once in Doha, the easiest way to get information is through your hotel's concierge.

Clockwise from top left: Museum Roundabout; Clock Tower monument; Al Zubara Fort

Local Knowledge

Climate

Qatar's climate is characterised by mild winters and very hot summers, with temperatures reaching over 40°C (104°F). Many residents choose to leave the country during July and August, as these are the hottest months of the year, as well as the most humid. In recent years the government has been trying to encourage people to stay in the country during the hot summer season by organising festivals that include shopping promotions and entertainment for families.

Doha's winter, from late October until late March, is pleasant during both the day and evening. Rainfall is scarce, averaging 70mm per year, falling on isolated days in winter.

Crime & Safety

Qatar is considered a safe country both for visitors and residents. The crime rate is much lower than in some western countries, but you should still take sensible precautions with valuables and cash, and avoid unfamiliar areas especially when alone or at night. Perhaps the biggest danger to the safety of visitors is the standard of driving on Qatar's roads. Accidents are commonplace, so expect the unexpected when driving, and be especially careful if out and about on foot.

Dos & Don'ts

Although there is a tolerance of other cultures in Qatar, you should remember that it's a Muslim country. In order to respect the culture and not offend the locals make sure you dress conservatively. For women, wearing tight clothes, sleeveless shirts and short skirts in public is frowned upon.

Public displays of intimacy between men and women are a no-no and can lead to arrest. Also, any form of contact between unmarried men and women is viewed unfavourably, so if in doubt when meeting a local of the opposite sex don't offer your hand unless it is offered first.

Alcohol is served here in very limited places and should never be drunk openly in public. You should not carry alcohol with you, even in your car. There is zero tolerance for drinking and driving. Depending on the circumstances, offenders may face detention, a substantial fine, a prison sentence or even deportation. Penalties for possession of drugs are severe, usually resulting in prison sentences. As for smoking, it is banned in government offices and major shopping malls.

Electricity & Water
The electricity in Qatar is 240 volts and the sockets are of the three-pin type, although most appliances will have two-pin plugs, so stock up on adaptors.

Tap water is safe to drink, but most expats drink mineral water, which you can either buy from the supermarket in boxes or have delivered in five-gallon bottles. These bottles can either be used with a water cooler or a pump. Water suppliers include Al Manhal (460 3332), Rayan Mineral Water (487 7662) and Safa International (460 6699).

Female Visitors
Women will face few problems or restrictions while in Qatar and are allowed to drive and travel freely (accompanied or alone). As with anywhere, local customs should be

respected and women should avoid tight or revealing clothing, especially when in traditional areas. No matter what, most females will find that they occasionally receive some unwanted stares, but it's best to ignore it if possible.

Language

The official language in Qatar is Arabic. It is used by locals and the relatively large Arab community residing here. The Arabic dialect used in Qatar is commonly dubbed Khaleeji, in reference to the Gulf (Al Khaleej). English is widely spoken and most road signs are written in both English and Arabic. English is widely used in tourist areas, hotels and malls. Urdu and Hindi are also commonly used in Qatar due to the huge community of south Asian workers.

Money

The monetary unit of Qatar is the Qatari riyal (QR). It is divided into 100 dirhams (not to be confused with the UAE dirham, which has almost the same value as the Qatari riyal). Banknote denominations include QR 1, QR 5, QR 10, QR 50, QR 100, and QR 500. The coins that are most commonly found are 25 and 50 dirhams. One, five, and 10 dirham coins are still legal tender but are rarely seen. The riyal is pegged to the US dollar at a rate of QR 3.65. Exchange rates of all major currencies are published daily in the local newspapers.

Cash is the preferred method of payment in Qatar, especially in smaller shops and the souks. Major shops, hotels and restaurants do take credit and debit cards. Cheques, however, are not widely accepted.

People With Disabilities

Facilities for disabled travellers are not as advanced as in some western countries but they are improving. Some hotels, such as the InterContinental, Four Seasons, Mövenpick, Ramada, Rydges Plaza, Sheraton and Ritz-Carlton, have rooms and facilities adapted for disabled guests, and the airport has ramps and chair lifts available. Doha International Airport's

Basic Arabic

General

Yes	na'am
No	la
Please	min fadlak (m)/min fadliki (f)
Thank you	shukran
Praise be to God	al-hamdu l-illah
God willing	in shaa'a l-laah

Greetings

Greeting (peace be upon you)	as-salaamu alaykom
Greeting (in reply)	wa alaykom is salaam
Good morning	sabah il-khayr
Good morning (in reply)	sabah in-nuwr
Good evening	masa il-khayr
Good evening (in reply)	masa in-nuwr
Hello	marhaba
Hello (in reply)	marhabtayn
How are you?	kayf haalak (m)/kayf haalik (f)
Fine, thank you	zayn, shukran (m)/zayna, shukran (f)

Welcome	ahlan wa sahlan
Goodbye	ma is-salaama
Introduction	
My name is...	ismiy...
What is your name?	shuw ismak (m) / shuw ismik (f)
Where are you from?	min wayn inta (m) / min wayn inti (f)
Questions	
How many / much?	kam?
Where?	wayn?
When?	mataa?
Which?	ayy?
How?	kayf?
What?	shuw?
Why?	laysh?
And	wa
Numbers	
Zero	sifr
One	waahad
Two	ithnayn
Three	thalatha
Four	arba'a
Five	khamsa
Six	sitta
Seven	saba'a
Eight	thamaanya
Nine	tiss'a
Ten	ashara

meet and greet service, Al Maha (465 6386), will also offer assistance to disabled visitors.

Police

The telephone number for the police (and all emergency services) is 999. The police are usually fairly quick to respond to a call. If you are involved in a minor traffic accident (that does not involve injury or major damage to the vehicle) you should move your vehicle to the side of the road, away from traffic, and wait until the police arrive. Police officers are generally courteous and professional, and always willing to offer assistance to visitors.

Telephone & Internet

Qatar has over 800 public phones, which can be operated for local and international calls using payphone cards that are available throughout the country. Qtel also offers two calling cards, the Qcard that can be used from any telephone, payphone or mobile, and the Dawli International Card with low international rates that can be used from any Qtel mobile or landline. Hala is a pay-as-you-talk option. Hala SIM cards are available at Qtel offices, and the scratch-off recharge cards (with values of QR 30, QR 50 and QR 100) are widely available in shops, supermarkets and Qtel offices. For more information visit the Qtel website (www.qtel.com.qa).

Qtel Wi-Fi HotSpots are all over the city, mainly in hotels and cafes, and also along the Corniche. Customers with a wireless-enabled laptop, PDA or mobile can buy prepaid HotSpot cards in denominations of QR 30, QR 50, and QR 70. There are several internet cafes scattered around Doha too (they charge around QR 6 per hour). You can also get 10 minutes' free internet access at the main Post Office. For a list of Qtel's Wi-Fi HotSpot locations, visit www.qtel.com.qa.

Time

Qatar local time is three hours ahead of UCT (Universal Coordinated Time – formerly known as GMT). It is fixed across the country and there is no summertime daylight saving. So when it is 12:00 in Doha, it is 13:00 in the UAE, 09:00 in London, 04:00 in New York, 18:00 in Tokyo, and 14:30 in New Delhi (not allowing for any daylight saving in those countries).

Dress Code

Qatar is a Muslim country, and as such you should respect the local customs by dressing conservatively whenever out in public. Skirts or shorts above the knee should be avoided, as should sleeveless tops that expose the shoulders or upper arms. Very tight or revealing clothing is a no-no (for men and women). It's not that you'll get into heaps of trouble, you'll just attract a lot of unwelcome attention and possibly some remarks.

Tipping

Tipping is not as regimented in this part of the world. Tips are most common in restaurants, averaging 10%, although some establishments automatically add a 10% service charge (this should be stated on the menu). Taxi fares are generally minimal so tips that round out dirhams or riyals are common. Tipping for tour guides is subjective, but is good practice.

Financial District

Newspapers & Magazines

The three main English newspapers are *Gulf Times, Qatar Tribune* and *The Peninsula*. They are published every day except for Friday, and cover a range of international and local issues. Each paper costs QR 2 and you can find them in supermarkets, shops, hotels, bookshops, and they are also sold by street vendors at traffic lights.

Some UAE-based English publications like the *Khaleej Times* and *Gulf News* are also available. Foreign newspapers, mostly British, American and Asian, are also available but they usually arrive 24 hours after the publication date. Imported English language magazines are often more expensive than their standard retail price, and are mostly hobby magazines. Many are censored using a black marker pen or by tearing out sections. There are three local Arabic dailies issued in Qatar: *Al-Raya, Al-Sharq* and *Al-Watan*, which cost QR 2.

Television

There are two television channels operated by Qatar Television – Channel One, which is in Arabic, and Channel Two, which is mostly in English. Qtel offers cable television (Qatar Cablevision) which supplies all available networks with one decoder. The system has a range of programmes suitable for both English and Arabic-speaking viewers, including STAR, Orbit, ART and Showtime.

Radio

There are only a few Qatar-based radio stations available. Qatar Radio (QBS) is the main station, which operates in both English and French on 97.5 FM and 102.6 FM. French programming is broadcast between 13:15 and 16:00. Arabic-speaking listeners can tune into Voice of the Gulf on 100.8 FM.

Books & Maps

A listing of Qatar's monthly events can be found in a free booklet called *Qatar Happening*, which is usually distributed in malls, hotels, and some DVD rental stores. There are very few travel guides on Qatar, but the locally published booklet *Marhaba* provides comprehensive listings and information about the country and tips for new residents. Another guidebook is a business travellers' handbook simply entitled *Qatar*, published by Gulf Agency Qatar. Explorer Publishing's *Impressions Qatar* is a coffee table photography book that captures the essence of the country. *Doha Mini Map* is a handy, pocket sized map which will help you navigate your way around Doha's roundabouts and elusive road names.

Websites & Blogs

www.cia.gov	Country profile
www.doha-online.com	Tourist information
www.experienceqatar.com	Photos, events, news, brochures
www.gov.qa	Qatar government online
www.thepeninsulaqatar.com	News, economic information, photos
www.qatarliving.com	What's on and community forum
http://english.aljazeera.net	Qatar and world news in English
http://english.mofa.gov.qa	Info on country, government, economy & tourism

Public Holidays & Annual Events

Public Holidays

The two major public holidays in Qatar are religious ones: Eid Al Fitr and Eid Al Adha. Eid Al Fitr marks the end of the fasting month of Ramadan, which is the ninth month of the Islamic calendar (Hijri calendar). During this month, Muslims are required to abstain from food, drink, cigarettes, sexual acts and unclean thoughts from dawn until dusk.

The Islamic calendar is based on the lunar months, so the beginning and the end of Ramadan is not fixed but it is decided instead on the sighting of the moon. As a result, religious holidays are only determined 24 hours in advance.

Eid Al Fitr is usually marked by a three-day celebration and many businesses in the country shut down. Eid Al Adha, the festival of the sacrifice, commemorates Ibrahim's willingness to sacrifice his son to God. It follows Eid Al Fitr by around 70 days and is marked by a four-day celebration. Besides these two religious celebrations there are two other fixed holidays: Accession Day, and National Day. Lailat Al Mi'raj celebrates the Prophet's ascension into heaven.

Public Holidays	
Prophet Muhammad's Birthday (1) (2009)	09 Mar (Moon)
Accession Day (1)	27 Jun (Fixed)
Lailat Al Mi'raj (1) (2009)	19 Jul (Moon)
Eid Al Fitr (3) (2009)	20 Sep (Moon)
Eid Al Adha (4) (2009)	20 Nov (Moon)
Islamic New Year (2009)	18 Dec (Moon)
National Day (1)	18 Dec (Fixed)

Traditional Qatari dance

Annual Events

Qatar Masters Golf Tournament   January
Doha Golf Club   www.qatar-masters.com

The Qatar Masters is an annual event on the PGA European tour. The Doha Golf Club has hosted the competition on its 18 hole course, which was designed by architect Peter Harradine, since 1998. The event attracts some of the world's best players who compete for a share of the $2.5 million prize money.

Qatar International
Tennis Tournaments   January to February
Khalifa Tennis Complex   www.qatartennis.org

Attracting top names every year, the ExxonMobil Open is the men's event held in January, and the Total Open is the women's tournament in mid February. Both are held at the home of the Qatar Tennis Federation. Doha will also host the Sony Ericsson Championship (www.sonyericsson-championships.com) in October and is set to stage the event until 2010.

Tour Of Qatar   January to February
The Corniche

Imagine the Tour de France in hotter weather – and in the desert. Part of Union Cycliste Internationale, which organises rides all over the world, this 710km ride through Qatar is now in its sixth year, and attracts big name riders (and bigger crowds).

Doha Cultural Festival
Various Locations

February to March
http://dohafestival.net

A week-long collection of cultural activities, from poetry readings to theatre performances, this annual festival celebrates the rich culture and history of Qatar. Several events take place across Doha, with the majority based in the Heritage Village. Visit the website for a detailed schedule of events.

Powerboat Racing
The Corniche

February to March
www.f1boat.com

Class 1 offshore powerboat racing is the fastest and most exhilarating of all watersports, and each year Qatar hosts two rounds of the world championship. Spectators can enjoy the action along Doha's Corniche and cheer on the local Qatar team, which despite being a relatively new entrant to the sport has already posted some impressive results.

Dunestock
Mesaieed

March or April
www.dunestock.net

Now in its fourth year, this outdoor music festival attracts a crowd of people for a different experience, the chance to dance in the dunes. The show features local musicians who come to showcase their talents, and there are also numerous food vendors on site making it a great place to spend a weekend. There are even showers onsite should you want to camp. The festival is usually held in March or April, in an area known as the 'Singing Sand Dunes', but check the website for details.

Motorbike Racing

April

Losail Motor Racing Circuit   www.circuitlosail.com

The brand new Losail motor racing circuit outside Doha is the venue for the Qatar Commercialbank Grand Prix, a leg of the MotoGP World Championship, in April. The circuit also hosts Superbike events and the Losail National Cup, and sometimes allows wannabe boy (and girl) racers to burn rubber on 'track days'. Visit the website for more information.

Doha Summer Festival

July to August

Various Locations   www.dohasummerfestival.com

Tarmac-melting temperatures often see expat families returning home for the summer, but for those who do stay, the Qatar Summer Wonders festival is an annual programme of family-friendly activities and events in the main shopping malls. The month-long festival also sees shops cutting their prices by up to 50%, making this a great time to do some serious bargain hunting while the kids are entertained.

Eid Al Fitr

20 September 2009 (moon)

Eid Al Fitr (the festival of the breaking of the fast) takes place at the end of the holy month of Ramadan. This occasion is often characterised by big family get-togethers and celebrations with feasts and gifts.

Eid Al Adha

20 November 2009 (moon)

Eid Al Adha (the festival of sacrifice) marks the end of the Hajj (the pilgrimage to Mecca). During this festival, people dress in new clothes and visit friends and family, and a sheep

Powerboat racing along the Corniche

will often be slaughtered to commemorate the time when Ibrahim was prepared to sacrifice his son to Allah.

Islamic New Year
18 December 2009 (moon)
Islamic New Year marks the start of the Islamic Hijri calendar, which is based on the lunar cycles. It should fall on 18 December in 2009, but can sometimes be announced a day or two earlier or later depending on the sighting of the moon.

National Day
18 December
This national celebration is a fairly recent addition to Qatar's public holidays and commemorates the assumption of power of Sheikh Jassem bin Mohamed bin Thani in 1868. Most government offices will be closed.

Getting Around

The car is king in Qatar; giant four-wheel drives hurtling down highways are the norm and many people pop behind the wheel simply to avoid the warm weather.

A good road network, and the absence of buses, trams and trains, means that getting from A to B involves getting behind the wheel. A series of north-south ring roads follow the shape of Doha's Corniche, while major routes head off north, south, and west to link the capital with the rest of the country. Taxis are fairly easy to find, particularly around hotels and malls.

The bus system in Doha is improving and relatively cheap for those that don't have a car. There is also a bus system that links many of Qatar's other cities with Doha. The warm weather and dubious driving can make it risky business for those who attempt to get around the city by bike.

Bicycle

While cycling the seven kilometres of the Corniche is popular, especially in the cooler months, there are no dedicated cycle tracks around the city. As a mode of transport to get you around the city, cycling is not a great choice. Thanks to the somewhat aggressive driving habits and heat, hopping on your bike to get to work is not an activity that is commonplace. There is however a cycling federation (www.qatarcf.org), which organises regular rides and races for those who are keen to get pedalling.

Boat

With so much coastline there is plenty for boat owners to see and do, but there are no regular passenger services linking coastal towns and cities. There was previously a ferry service between Iran and Qatar, operated by the Qatar National Navigation Company, but this has been halted indefinitely. It is possible to take a boat ride to some of the offshore islands or to cruise the bay aboard a traditional dhow. The best bet is to contact one of the local tour operators for island tours.

Bus

There is a public bus service throughout most neighbourhoods in Doha and to other major cities. The Al Ghanim Bus Station is located off of Grand Hamad Street in the middle of the city. The station is currently more of a depot for buses to come and go but this is made up for by the modern, clean, air conditioned buses. The Karwa bus service is managed by Mowasalat. The bus fare is QR 2 for a single trip. Unlimited day, week and monthly passes are available for QR 6, QR 30 and QR 120 respectively. Single and day tickets can be purchased on most buses. Current bus fares, route maps and instructions can be found at eng.mowasalat.com.

Driving & Car Hire

The country has a good network of roads and highways, generally in a decent state of repair. However, Doha's many roundabouts can be daunting and confusing, and the burgeoning population is leading to increased congestion and traffic delays in the capital.

Signposts are almost always in English as well as Arabic. Petrol stations can be found throughout Doha and along the main roads in Qatar, and most visitors will be pleasantly surprised to find the price of fuel is a lot lower than elsewhere in the world. This means that many motorists can afford to run gas-guzzling 4WDs, of which there are many on Qatar's roads.

If you intend to drive in Qatar you must have your wits about you and remain alert at all times, as speeding, tail-gating, and sudden lane-changing are all too common. Be careful to contain your frustration though, as obscene gestures and examples of road-rage can result in severe penalties. Driving is on the right, and seatbelts are mandatory for the driver and front seat passenger. A further hazard to be aware of when driving outside the towns is camels crossing the road.

In order to lease a car, you will need a credit card, a copy of your passport and a valid driving licence. There are a number of reputable leasing companies in Doha, many of which are internationally recognised. Some companies have branches at the airport. The longer the leasing period, the better the discount you will be given on the price. The monthly rate for leasing a car starts at QR 1,600 and QR 3,500 for a 4WD.

Taxi

If you're planning to stay in Doha for a long visit, then relying on taxis may be a pain. At times it seems like there are not enough and if you're unlucky you may end up waiting a while for one. At the moment there are two types of taxis, the run-down orange-and-white ones and the new (more expensive) blue cars. The future plan is that the Karwa taxis will eventually replace the orange-and-white ones which are being withdrawn from the market gradually. The good news is that Karwa is steadily increasing its number of cars, so there should be more taxis out and about.

Karwa taxis' meters start at QR 4 and run at QR 1.25 per kilometre. Taxis picked up outside hotels will often charge a premium rate. To save yourself from having to flag a taxi, you can always order one in advance for an extra charge of QR 4 by calling 458 8888. There is no central dispatch to order a car from for the orange-and-white taxis, so your only option is to flag one down. Taxi drivers know the city pretty well, although

Car Rental Agencies

AAB Rent-A-Car Company	431 4469
Al Muftah Rent a Car	444 2003
Al Sulaiman Rent a Car	435 5477
Alfardan Automobiles	460 1177
Avis	466 7744
Budget Car & Van Rental	431 0411
Elite Limo	442 6184
Europcar	466 0677
Hertz Rent A Car	467 7829
Mannai Autorent	455 8636
National Car Rental	436 6881
Prestige Rent a Car	483 8500
Sixt Rent A Car	493 3350

street names are not commonly used and most drivers navigate using landmarks.

Taking a taxi from the airport, you have the option of either an orange-and-white taxi whose driver will refuse to take you anywhere for less than QR 20 to QR 30, or taking a blue taxi which uses meters but has a higher pick-up charge from the airport.

Walking

Perhaps because of the summer heat, or maybe because everybody can afford a luxury car, walking is not a common mode of transport in Qatar. Modern roads, ample parking and cars equipped with super-cool air-conditioning make driving a much more pleasant way to get around. However, there are plenty of areas suitable for those who walk for pleasure – the famous Corniche, which runs a 7km stretch from the Sheraton to Ras Abu Abboud, is always busy with active people striding, biking, rollerblading or pram-pushing up and down.

Further Out

To explore remote areas around Doha, you may want to hire a 4WD or join an organised tour (p.92). There are a few heritage sites, museums, forts and fishing villages around the country. Al Wakrah (p.5), Umm Salal (p.90) and Al Zubara (p.87) all have interesting sites that are worth visiting if you are in the area, but it is good to join organised tours as you may venture out only to find forts and towers are closed for renovation.

Out and about in Qatar

Places To Stay

Qatar's growing range of premium hotels provide a serving of glamour to visitors arriving in the region for business or pleasure.

Several hotels are either under construction or at the planning stage; during 2008 an estimated 12,000 new rooms were being built as Qatar increased its bid for a stronger tourism sector. Qatar promotes itself as a high-quality destination, appealing to well-off tourists, business travellers, and the lucrative Mice market (meetings, incentives, conferences and exhibitions). Luxury four and five-star hotels dominate the accommodation options, although there are also a number of reasonably priced hotels out there. Another alternative is to book into a serviced hotel apartment (see p.49), which tends to work out cheaper than hotels for longer stays. At the moment there are no hostels to speak of, or camping resorts, although camping is popular in the cooler months (see p.92).

Most five-star hotels are located in the West Bay, which is the area that has the most beaches. Occupancy rates in Doha's hotels are very high, as visitor numbers (both business visitors and tourists) are increasing faster than new hotels can be built. More expensive hotels usually provide direct access to the beach and comprehensive sports facilities, a spa and a collection of restaurants. Nearly all of the popular western chains are represented in the city. New additions to the luxury hotel scene include a new W Hotel (p.47), and St Regis, which is set to open in 2010.

Ezdan Hotel & Suites

www.ezdanhotels.com

496 9111

Centrally located near West Bay, Ezdan accommodates business travellers with its fully furnished suites. A personal assistant, meeting centre, spa and kids' club are some of the services on offer. Map 3 C3

Four Seasons Hotel

www.fourseasons.com/doha

494 8888

This 232 room hotel is vying for the crown of Qatar's finest hotel. The Four Seasons has an exclusive beach and marina and first-class service which should impress cosmopolitan visitors. Map 3 F2

InterContinental Doha

www.intercontinental.com/doha

484 4444

This hotel is known for having the longest beach and largest free-form pool in town. It is located outside of the city, about 25 minutes from the airport. The hotel also features top-notch restaurants. Map 2 E2

La Cigale

www.lacigalehotel.com

428 8888

A short ride from the airport, La Cigale features exclusive amenities. The new hotel has a reputation for first-class hospitality. It has five restaurants, including live cooking stations at Le Cigalon. Map 4 D2

Ramada Plaza Doha

www.ramadaplazadoha.com

428 1428

This is a large capacity hotel offers cable TV and high speed internet access from its central location. Facilities include a large swimming pool, gym, tennis courts a business centre and popular restaurants. Map 4 D2

The Ritz-Carlton Doha

www.ritzcarlton.com/doha

484 8000

The Ritz features exquisitely decorated rooms with breathtaking views. You can enjoy watersports, and a good mix of spa treatments at this hotel and the restaurants serve International and Arabic cuisine. Map 2 E1

Places To Stay

Sealine Beach Resort

www.qnhc.com

412 8086

About 55km from Doha Airport, the
Sealine Beach Resort is an escape from
Doha's ongoing construction. Set in
picturesque gardens, the hotel has
guest rooms, intimate chalets for two,
and villas for up to six people.

Sharq Village & Spa

www.sharqvillage.com

425 6666

Sharq Village & Spa is reminiscent of
a traditional Qatari village, but with
all the modern-day elegance and
facilities. On site are the flagship Six
Senses Spa (p.121) and Al Dana (p.194)
restaurant along the beach. Map 4 F2

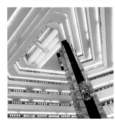

Sheraton Doha Hotel & Resort

www.sheraton.com/doha

485 4444

Overlooking the Corniche, the
Sheraton has a good range of sports
facilities and restaurants. Alongside
acres of landscaped gardens, the hotel
also has access to the beach. Map 3 F3

Somerset West Bay, Doha

www.somerset.com

420 3456

Located in the Diplomatic area, this hotel is convenient for those here on business, and its kitted-out serviced apartments offer views of the Arabian Gulf. Facilities include a swimming pool, sauna and gym. Map 3 E1

W Hotel & Residences

www.whotels.com

499 6530

The new W Hotel adds contemporary style to Qatar's conservative luxury hotel scene. The swanky hotel's decor is minimalism at its best and the chain swears by its superior service. Map 3 D1

Marriott Doha

www.dohamarriott.com

429 8888

Located a few minutes from the airport, this modern hotel is favoured by business travellers as it provides a wide range of facilities. Its restaurants are popular and the view from the rooftop is worth a photo or two. Map 4 F2

Hotel Apartments

The cost of renting a furnished hotel apartment can be cheaper in the long term than a standard hotel room. The daily rate for a one-bed apartment is around QR 400, while the monthly rate for a two-bed should be between QR 8,000 and QR 12,000. Most buildings have some kind of leisure facilities for guests, although perhaps not as comprehensive as the big hotels.

Campsites

Camping is not a regulated activity in Qatar, and as such there are no official campsites with facilities. However, camping takes place on a regular basis by residents and locals and is certainly a part of local tradition. For expatriates living in Qatar, it is perhaps best to take a cautionary approach unless invited by a local. A number of local tour operators provide organised camping trips that include meals and entertainment among the sand dunes (see p.92 for a list of tour operators).

Hotel Apartments

Al-Muntazah		
Plaza Hotel	Al Muntazah	435 5677
Gulf Paradise	Al Sadd	432 2212
Retaj Residence	Al Hitmi Al Jadeed	489 5555
Royal Wings	Najma	421 1333
Sahara Hotel	Al Hitmi	432 7771
Somerset West Bay	Diplomatic District	420 3456

Exploring

52 Explore Qatar

54 Al Sadd &
Al Rayyan Road

58 Diplomatic Area
& West Bay

64 Doha Corniche

70 Khalifa Street
& Al Luqta Street

74 Salwa Road
& Al Aziziyah

80 Souk Area &
Souk Waqif

86 Outside of Doha

92 Tours & Sightseeing

Explore Qatar

In its bid to become the cultural capital of the Middle East, Qatar has developed a network of world-class museums and archaeological sites.

Qatar's bizarre mix of barren desert, expansive coast, and booming urban sprawl makes for an exciting place to investigate. For the historically oriented traveller, archaeological sites abound both in and out of the capital, Doha, and the government has taken great care in preserving the country's surprisingly detailed past. Art and architecture buffs are equally catered for – the newly opened Museum of Islamic Art (p.64) has already established itself as the premiere cultural destination in the region, and the ever-ascending skyscrapers in the Diplomatic District (p.58) wouldn't seem out of place in a science fiction novel.

The vast majority of Qatar's population lives in Doha and most of the country's attractions are there as well. The city revolves around the Corniche-lined bay. At the south end of the bay lies Doha International Airport. Working north around the bay, you'll find the souk area (p.80), which includes the accurately restored Souk Waqif. Follow the Corniche even further and you'll soon find yourself among the towering skyscrapers of the Diplomatic Area. The Corniche itself (p.64) is a major attraction and a walk along it, if the climate's right, is a must for any visitor.

Travelling south west from the souks you'll run into the shop-lined Salwa Road (p.74). Head north from Salwa Road

Mosque and reflecting pool

to reach two of Doha's newest institutions: the Villaggio Mall (p.135) and Aspire Park (p.75), which hosted many of the events of the 2006 Asian Games. Directly north of Aspire lies Education City (p.71).

To finish the loop, drive east on Al Luqta Street and Khalifa Street to witness another of the city's main thoroughfares. This corridor will take you back to the Corniche, where you'll be greeted by the skyscrapers of the Diplomatic District.

Each area in this chapter is linked to a corresponding section in the Going Out chapter (p.144). This way, you'll be able to plan your meals in accordance with your travels. When trying to navigate, be warned: street maps usually show the Corniche and bay at the top, which is logical, but the bay is actually in the east of the city, not the north, as often implied.

Al Sadd & Al Rayyan Road

Travelling through old Qatar, Al Rayyan Road and its surrounding areas are a visual treat for first time visitors to the Gulf.

Named after the suburb to which it leads, Al Rayyan Road has long been a main artery through Doha. The roundabout-laden thoroughfare starts at the east end of the city, near the souks, and travels west past the new Medical City and Education City. Al Sadd Street, which runs parallel to Al Rayyan Road, is a busy commercial area with restaurants and shops, including the Royal Plaza shopping mall (p.137). Running between Al Rayyan and Al Sadd is Jawaan Street, which has the Grand Regency and Millennium hotels as well as Centrepoint shopping mall (p.135). *For restaurants and bars in the area, see p.154.*

Al Wajbah Fort
Nr Emir's Palace, Al Rayyan

With its high towers and thick walls, this fort is considered one of the oldest in the country. It was the site of a famous battle in 1893, when the people of Qatar defeated the Ottoman forces. As a result, the name of Al Wajbah evokes a strong feeling of pride among local people. To reach the fort, turn off the roundabout before the Emir's palace (if driving from Doha), go over the speed bumps and turn right at the end of the gravel track. Entry is free.

Fahd Bin Ali Palace

Al Rayyan Rd, nr Emiri Diwan, Al Amir

The palace has a permanent exhibition of coins and blown-up old photographs of Doha, as well as various temporary exhibitions. The black-and-white photographs are fascinating and there are some good aerial shots dating back to 1947, when Doha was little more than a small cluster of buildings by the sea; they progress through to the present. There are also some great shots of pearl fishermen in the late 1950s and the first oil rig in Dukhan.

Fun City   428 9251

Centrepoint, Al Sadd

This small but nicely maintained soft play area has a separate section with dressing-up clothes, slides and a drawing table. You pay per hour for the play areas and the small rides cost extra. There's also a kids' hairdressers upstairs. Parents suffer, though, because there are only three chairs. Map 4 C2

Ray's Reef   413 0000

Royal Plaza, Al Sadd   www.royalplazadoha.com

This new play place has a bright nautical theme and a small cafe. It has two adventure play areas with tunnels, slides and cannons for firing balls from the ball pool. There's also a home corner and a TV area with plush red velvet step seating. Creative kids can make use of the easels and paints. For a fixed price, children can play with what they like, but the many arcade games cost extra. Map 4 C2

If you only do one thing in...
Al Sadd & Al Rayyan Road

Take a trip to the Fahd Bin Ali Palace (p.55) to check out the old black and white photographs of Qatar. You'll be amazed at how far the country has come.

Best for...

Culture: Visit Al Wajbah fort, one of the oldest in the country and a piece of heritage that the locals are very proud of.

Drinking: Have a cocktail at Sky View (p.161). The posh views are worth every penny.

Eating: It's not pretty, but if you're new to the Middle East, you can't leave without tasting an authentic shawarma from Automatic (p.157).

Families: Take the kids to Ray's Reef (p.55). They can let loose while you relax at the cafe.

Sightseeing: Starting near the souks, Al Rayyan Road is long and well worth a drive. The ageing buildings are worth a snapshot or two.

Clockwise from top left: Typical barber shop, street food, Al Wajbah Fort

Diplomatic Area & West Bay

Once a Doha backwater, the northern part of the city has come to define the entire country's quick-paced development.

Cranes, freshly paved roads and futuristic skyscrapers announce your arrival into the Diplomatic Area of Doha. What was once a distant outcrop of the main city, this tiny peninsula on the north side of the bay has become the centre of Doha's incredible development. Several top hotels are located here, as is City Center Doha (p.134), the country's most famous mall and meeting place. Further north lies the West Bay, home to the Pearl Qatar (p.60) as well as the soon-to-be completed Cultural Village, which will house venues for both fine art and performing art. *For **bars and restaurants** in the area, see p.162.*

Aladdin's Kingdom   483 1001
Nr InterContinental Hotel, West Bay
Visit this ageing fairground on a weeknight and you might just have the place to yourself. Some of the big rides are closed during the week, but it gets busier at weekends. Despite the best efforts of the staff, it feels somewhat surreal and you half expect Scooby Doo to arrive ready to solve a mystery. Map 2 E2

INet Café   493 3312
City Center Doha, Diplomatic District   www.inetcafe.qa
A dark and noisy den for teenage gaming fans, INet offers network gaming and internet access for all ages. Enthusiasts

Qatar Financial Centre

can play each other or go online. Despite being called a cafe it offers no refreshments, so you'll have to tear yourself away from the games to grab a drink elsewhere. There are no arcade games or other attractions here, but it should keep computer gaming fanatics happy for hours. Map 3 D2

The Pearl Qatar

West Bay   www.thepearlqatar.com

This is Qatar's largest foray into the man-made island trend that has come to define many cities in the Gulf. Once completed, it will act as a self-sustaining city, with shops and restaurants, as well as housing and commercial space. Currently, the main attraction is the island itself. It's worth a visit just to experience the engineering marvel. Map 2 F1

Sheraton Gardens

At the north end of the Corniche, just before the Sheraton Hotel, this pleasant park provides great views across Doha Bay. There's plenty of parking available in the carpark or on the road nearby, and you'll find a kiosk selling juices, warm drinks and snacks. Map 3 E3

Winter Wonderland

City Center Doha   483 9163

This ice rink is located in the middle of City Center and can be seen from each floor. Open every day, 90 minutes of skating costs QR 35. Spectators can pay QR 10 to watch from the sidelines, which is unnecessary considering you can get a better view for free from the first floor balcony. Map 3 D2

Qtel Tower, Diplomatic Area

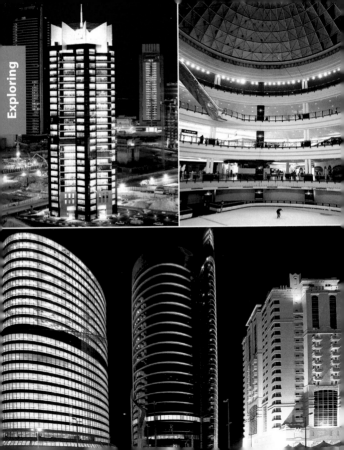

If you only do one thing in...

Diplomatic Area & West Bay

Hop in a rental car and spend the day gazing at the growing skyscrapers. It's not every day you get to see a city being constructed before your eyes.

Best for...

Drinking: Head to the basement of the Sheraton for a pint of Guinness at the Irish Harp (p.169).

Eating: Don't leave Doha without trying one of its fine dining options, and the contemporary Italian served at Il Teatro (p.166) is truly world class.

Families: Take the kids ice skating at Doha City Center (p.134).

Outdoor: Grab a juice from the tiny cafe and take in the panoramic views from Sheraton Gardens (p.172).

Sightseeing: Head north to the Pearl Qatar (p.60) and witness the country's most impressive development.

Doha Corniche

The heart of the city, Doha's perfectly manicured Corniche was purpose-built for late-night strolls and peaceful people watching.

Doha revolves around its gorgeously landscaped Corniche. Running along the length of the bay, the road starts at the impressive Sharq Village & Spa (p.47) in the south and ends up at the Sheraton Doha in the northern Diplomatic Area (p.47). Several of the country's top museums line the curving boulevard, including the newly finished Museum of Islamic Art, which has already become a cultural beacon in the region. One of the Corniche's greatest assets is its walkability. In a city consisting mainly of highways, the tree-lined path along the sea presents a perfect opportunity for experiencing a city that is usually seen through a windscreen. *For bars and restaurants in the area, see p.162.*

Museum Of Islamic Art

The Corniche

422 4444
www.mia.org.qa

Architect IM Pei has created an elegant home for this impressive collection. The building is subtle yet beautiful, with details drawn from a wide range of Islamic influences. The collection is showcased as a journey through time, countries and cultures, and the oldest piece dates from the ninth century. Along with the permanent and temporary galleries, there is a library and an auditorium where regular talks and interactive workshops are held. Map 5 D1

Museum Of Islamic Art

Museum Park
Nr Qatar National Museum
Next to the currently closed Qatar National Museum, and overlooking the Corniche, this large grassy area stretches for quite a distance. It has lots of play equipment and a big paved area, which is great for cycling and skateboarding. There is plenty of space for running around and enjoying picnics. There aren't many trees, however, so the park is more enjoyable in the evenings and during the cooler winter months. Map 5 F2

Qatar National Museum
444 2191

Museum Park St, Al Salata
www.qnm.8m.com

The museum has been under renovation for a number of months and is scheduled to reopen to the public in the near future. It showcases various coins, jewellery, traditional clothing, household items and tools. There are areas that recreate Bedouin scenes, as well as an exhibit on the oil industry. An aquarium contains marine creatures native to local shores. Map 5 F2

Rumeilah Park (Al Bidda Park)
Al Rumaila East, opposite Corniche
Located opposite the Corniche, this beautifully landscaped park tends to be busiest on Fridays and in the evenings. It has an amphitheatre and an area called the Heritage Village, that was built to resemble a traditional village. There are a few shops that open sporadically, and well-maintained toilets. A gallery, displaying work by local artists, is open 09:00 to 12:00 and 16:00 to 21:00. Map 4 D1

If you only do one thing in...
Doha Corniche

Head straight to the Museum of Islamic Art. The perfectly executed museum is already being hailed as the best cultural attraction in the region.

Best for...

Drinking: Sip on Arabic coffee and watch the dhows float through the bay at Balhambar (p.173).

Eating: Head to Ras Al Nasaa (p.174) and opt for a table at the Qasr Al Sahel Iranian restaurant, where you can dine on some of the best kebabs in Doha.

Families: If the weather's right, spend a day at Rumeilah Park and let the kids wander while you enjoy the bay breeze.

Outdoor: A trip to Doha isn't complete without a stroll along the well-groomed Corniche.

Sightseeing: The section of the Corniche in front of the Ministry of Interior (Map 5 B1) provides the best photo opportunities of the rising skyline.

Top: Marina in Doha, Bottom: Qatar National Museum

Khalifa Street & Al Luqta Street

Running directly into the gorgeously designed Education City, this main corridor eventually cuts through the country to the west coast.

Beginning at the Oryx Roundabout near the Corniche, Khalifa Street runs directly west out of the city and eventually turns into Al Luqta Street. Inside Doha proper, the corridor is home to Al Jazeera and Qatar TV, but things don't start to get interesting until the city starts to thin out, giving way to the gorgeous Education City (p.71), Al Shaqab Stud (p.70) and eventually the Sheikh Faisal Bin Qassim Al Thani Museum.

*For **restaurants and bars** in the area, see p.176.*

Al Shaqab Stud

480 6111
Nr Education City   www.alshaqabstud.com

Owned by Sheikh Hamad bin Khalifa Al Thani, this farm provides the opportunity for viewing gorgeous thoroughbred Arabian horses, many of which are world champions. Located behind Al Rayyan Football Club and next to Education City, there's also a riding school for all ages and abilities. Visits can be arranged directly or through one of the local tour operators. Map 1 B3

Dahal Al Hamam Park

Al Markiyah Street

Located on the corner of Arab League Street and Al Markiyah Street, this sizeable park has lots of grass and an enormous paved area. There is a cafe selling snacks and drinks that opens after

17:00. The family only park opens from 07:30 until midnight, so you can picnic and play until well after bedtime. Map 2 B3

Education City

Al Luqta Street   www.qf.edu.qa

Driving into Education City from the relatively barren area surrounding it is a somewhat surreal experience. Windblown desert speckled with dull, box-shaped buildings immediately transforms into lush lawns lined with some of the most tasteful, contemporary architecture in the Middle East. The massive complex is a cornerstone of the Qatar Foundation's master plan, and some of the world's best universities are represented here, including Cornell and Goergetown. You'll need a pass to access the buildings' interiors, but it's worth it just to drive around and gaze at the architecture. Map 1 A3

Sheikh Faisal Bin Qassim
Al Thani Museum   486 9966

Shahaniyah   www.fbqmuseum.com

Sheikh Faisal's personal collection, housed at his farm near Al Shahaniya, is considered by many to be one of the best museums in the country. Located inside a huge rectangular fort complex, it is home to a large collection of Islamic art, ancient weaponry, vintage cars, regional artefacts and rare books and manuscripts. One corner of the museum recreates a traditional Qatari house. To visit the museum you have to ring in advance to make arrangements. It's easy to get there by car, and unusually for Qatar it is signposted, but you can also ask one of Doha's tour companies (p.92) to arrange a visit.

If you only do one thing in...

Khalifa Street & Al Luqta Street

Drive through Education City (p.71). Call one of the universities in advance to get permission to view the interiors.

Best for...

Culture: Although it's a bit of a drive, Sheikh Faisal's personal museum is incredibly educational and worth the trip.

Eating: Dine on some of Doha's finest Indian food at Bukhara (p.177).

Families: Call ahead and take your kids to see the beautiful Arabian horses at Al Shaqab Stud (p.70).

Outdoor: Despite only being open to families, Dahal Al Hamam Park (p.70) is one of the nicest in the city and stays open until midnight every night.

Sightseeing: Although you can't take a tour without knowing someone on the inside, it's worth driving past the Al Jazeera headquarters on Khalifa Street just to see the hub of Arab media.

Salwa Road & Al Aziziyah

Whether you're looking for energetic nightlife or a fun place to take the family, Salwa Road fits the bill.

Starting at Doha's unofficial nightlife hub, the Ramada Plaza, Salwa is another of Doha's main arteries. Several of the city's most popular restaurants line the wide street, as do many of the old souks, including the animal, fish and vegetable markets. Drive far enough and you'll no doubt run into the Aspire complex, which hosted most of the events in the 2006 Asian Games. Directly after the Fish Market sits the area of Al Aziziyah, which is home to both the Villaggio Mall (p.135) and Hyatt Plaza (p.136). *For restaurants and bars in the area, see p.178.*

Al Muntazah Park

C Ring Road

This is one of the older parks in Doha, and has large grassy areas and mature trees. Located at the corner of the C Ring Road and Al Muntazah Street, the park is only accessible to women and children (boys up to the age of nine), and tends to be busiest in the evenings and at the end of the week. Entrance is free of charge. The park is currently closed for renovation. Map 4 D3

Animal Souk

Salwa Rd, Al Waab

This is one of the few places in Qatar that will truly make you feel like an outsider. Western visitors are rare, but the vendors are friendly and eager to talk to you, although their English is often very basic. In case you are interested, a young camel will set you back around QR 5,000, and you can get an adult one for QR 10,000 upwards. Sheep and goats go for about QR 500 each, and if you pay a bit extra the sellers will prepare the animal for eating. Taking photos of the vendors and their merchandise shouldn't be a problem, just make sure you ask first. Map 4 B4

Aspire Academy

413 6000
www.aspire.qa

Nxt to Villaggio Mall

Thanks in part to the 2006 Asian Games, Doha now sports a world-class athletics compound. The two main attractions here are the Aspire Tower and the Khalifa International Stadium. At the time of writing, neither was open to visitors, although you might be able to tour of Khalifa International Stadium by getting in touch with Aspire Academy (p.75). Either way, both structures are monuments in their own right and worth a visit. Map 4 A3

Aspire Park

Next to Aspire Academy

Doha's largest park covers 88 hectares (the size of more than 80 football pitches) and has a large lake, jogging track, shaded seating areas, a restaurant and plenty of parking. Although more than 700 trees have been planted, there is not an overabundance of shade, so try to visit after sundown or during the cooler months. Map 4 A3

Doha Zoo
458 5858

Al Furousiya St, Salwa Road South

Although it's well-maintained, the Doha Zoo is a bit old-fashioned. It has about 1,500 animals including lions, an elephant and giraffes. The larger animals do not seem to have much space and seem less than happy. Tuesdays are for women and children only and Wednesdays for families.
Map 1 A4

Fish Market

Salwa Rd, Al Maamoura

This is not a place for those with weak stomachs; the odour is quite intense, but think of it as a cultural adventure. The air-conditioned market opens at 04:00 and the early morning is the best time for photographs since the fish bins are usually full and local restaurant buyers are abundant. Most of the vendors speak limited English, but are happy to try to explain the catch of the day. Well worth a visit if you like witnessing more 'authentic' ways of life. Map 4 B4

Gondolania
450 7873

Villaggio Mall, Al Aziziyah

This new and exotically named ice rink is in the middle of the food court at Villaggio Mall. Coaches are usually around to give you a hand and you can also book private lessons. The whole rink is occasionally used for ice hockey tournaments or private events. It costs QR 30 for a 105 minute session. Map 4 A3

Goat seller at the Animal Souk

Jungle Zone

469 4848

Hyatt Plaza, Al Aziziyah   www.hyattplaza.com

This children's area has nine attractions that are all themed around the jungle world. It is located in the foodcourt so parents can eat and let the children play all in one spot. Prices are QR 45 at weekends (Thursday to Saturday) and QR 30 during the week. Map 4 A3

Qatar National Heritage Library

487 0427

Off Al Luqta St, nr D Ring Rd

This collection of 85,000 books, manuscripts, maps and scientific instruments are housed in a large villa on a quiet side street. One of the highlights is a rare set of volumes detailing Napoleon's expedition to Egypt in 1798. The museum is intended for historians and researchers, but they are happy to give tours if you call in advance. Map 2 B4

If you only do one thing in...

Salwa Road & Al Aziziyah

Bargain for a baby goat at the animal souk (p.74). Visitors are rare here so you'll see an untainted view of old Doha.

Best for...

Drinking: The Ramada Plaza is full drinking holes, but Bubbles (p.190) is probably the most fun.

Culture: If the Animal Souk isn't 'culturally intense' enough for you, head to the fish market to experience Doha's other sights and smells.

Eating: For the best Lebanese in town, head straight to Layali Restaurant (p.186).

Families: Aspire Park (p.75) is perfect for a relaxing day outdoors. Kids will have more than enough space to roam.

Sightseeing: Drive through Aspire Academy (p.75) to get a glimpse of Khalifa Stadium and the Aspire Tower.

Souk Area & Souk Waqif

The cultural capital of Qatar, Souk Waqif's stone walls and cobbled alleyways house some of Doha's best-kept secrets.

Doha's souk area has long been the centre of activity for the country. Rural Bedouins used to travel to the market to sell their milk, meat and crafts. The city's oldest market, Souk Waqif, was renovated in 2004 using traditional building methods and materials. The resulting complex is now one of the most beautiful and authentic modern souks in the Gulf. The most refreshing aspect of the souk area is its dual purpose – tourists can easily stroll the narrow alleys in search of souvenirs while locals can purchase everything from fishing nets to pots and pans. *For restaurants and bars in the area, see p.192.*

Doha Fort (Al Koot Fort)   442 4143

Nxt to Souk Waqif, Al Jasra

This white Moorish-style fort, next to Souk Waqif (p.130), is being restored so it is not open to the public at the moment. Located on the corner of Jasim bin Mohammed and Al Qalaa streets, it was built in 1927 to protect the souk from thieves. It is one of the few remaining military forts in Doha. One of the more fascinating features of the structure is the roofless, wall-less mosque that sits in the courtyard. Map 5 C2

Waqif Art Center

Orientalist Museum

Off Al Muthaf St, Al Salata

436 7711
izzam@qma.com.qa

This small white building is home to an impressive collection of Orientalist paintings and drawings, showing life in the Arab world in the 19th century. The paintings were collected by Sheikh Hassan bin Mohammed Al Thani over 15 years, and he donated them in 2005. To view the paintings you need to make an appointment by calling 583 6574. To get to the museum, turn right at the Perfume Pots Roundabout on the Corniche past Qatar National Museum, take the first right and the museum is on your left. Map 5 E2

The Third Line

Waqif Art Center

434 0921
www.thethirdline.com

This gallery started out in Dubai, and the Doha branch is its second location. It specialises in showing contemporary artists and photographers from the Middle East, as well as North Africa and the Far East. The gallery launched with an exhibition by Egyptian photographer Youssef Nabil, showing his quirky but powerful hand-coloured prints. The gallery itself is pretty small but it's a big deal for Doha to have a proper space showing modern work, and the Waqif Art Center is the perfect home for it. Map 5 C2

Waqif Art Center

Souk Waqif, Al Jasra

660 5841
www.waqifartcenter.com

The Waqif Art Center is home to several small galleries and shops. With constantly changing exhibitions, it covers sculpture, photography and paintings. There are also several

Souk Waqif

trendy shops selling original art and calligraphy, books, designer house stuff, antiques and unique and funky clothes. It also runs various courses dealing with everything from art appreciation to drawing and video art. Map 5 C2

Windtower House
Off Grand Hamad & Ali bin Abdulla St

This is one of the last traditional windtowers in Qatar. You will find it off Grand Hamad Street and Ali bin Abdullah Street, enclosed within the downmarket Najada Shopping Plaza. Windtowers, known as barjeel in Arabic, were used in the days before electricity as a primitive form of air conditioning. They work by sucking fresh cool air into a house. Map 5 D2

If you only do one thing in...
Souk Area & Souk Waqif

Just walk. Souk Waqif's renovation was so well-executed that it warrants at least a day of wondering.

Best for...

Culture: The Third Line (p.82) showcases contemporary Middle Eastern artists, a rarity in this part of the world.

Drinking: Sip a smooth scotch while you relax at the sophisticated Cigar Lounge (p.170).

Eating: Book a teppanyaki table at Asia Live! (p.195) and marvel at the culinary entertainment.

Families: Walk the kids to Doha Fort (p.80) and let them imagine the history that took place there.

Outdoor: Head to the upstairs terrace at Tajine (p.200) to sample some subtle Moroccan flavours, while enjoying the cool bay breeze.

Top: shops in Souk Waqif, Bottom: Al Koot Fort

Outside of Doha

Amateur archaeologists will love exploring the barren expanses and fort-littered coasts. Rent a car, bring a map and enjoy the solitude.

Although the majority of Qatar's attractions are located in and around Doha, a trip through the desert allows visitors a chance to see a more traditional side of the country. The north-west coast is littered with old fortifications and empty stone houses. Places like Al Zubara (p.88) are filled with remnants of 'old Qatar', including the Zubara fort (p.88). It's also worth taking a trip into the desert, especially if you're heading to the Inland Sea (p.90) in the south of the peninsula. If vacant beaches are your thing, head west towards Ras Abrouq, just north of Dukhan, which offers great, empty sandy beaches.

Al Jassasiyeh

Al Huwailah, Northern Qatar

These rocky hills that overlook the north-eastern coast of Qatar, between the two villages of Al Huwailah and Fuwairit, contain more than 900 prehistoric carvings depicting different types of boats. The carvings also show rows of cup marks or depressions, believed by some to have been used for traditional games called al aailah and al haloosah. Others believe that the depressions were designed simply to catch rain water. The area is difficult to find, so you may want to arrange a trip through a tour company.

Inside the fort tower at Umm Salal Mohammed

Al Khor Museum

472 1866

Al Khor Corniche, North of Doha

The rooms on the ground floor of Al Khor Museum showcase the fishing, pearling and dhow building industries, while the upper floor displays archaeological finds from the neolithic and bronze ages. There's a shaded area next to the museum with a playground and views of the harbour and sea. After visiting the museum, drive further along the Corniche and visit the old watchtowers that still stand guard over the town.

Al Rakiyat Fort

Al Rakiyat, Northern Qatar

This fort was built between the 17th and 19th centuries, and restored in 1988. It is made of stone and mud and, similar

to other forts in the country, is rectangular with a tower at each corner. The fort is located near a camel farm, just off the coastal road between Al Zubara and Madinat Al Shamal. You'll have to drive off-road for a few hundred metres but it is possible in a normal car. The site is open to the public, but apart from the building itself there's little else to see.

Al Zubara Fort

Al Zubara, Northern Qatar

Built in 1938, during the reign of Sheikh Abdullah bin Jassim Al Thani, this fort was erected beside the ruins of a much older fort. The impressive structure is square in shape, with high, thick walls, and has circular towers in three of its corners. The fort once served as a coastguard station and, until the mid 1980s, it was still being used by the military. It is a long drive from Doha, along rather bumpy roads, so it is probably better to visit this fort if you're already in the area.

Al Zubara Town

Al Zubara, Northern Qatar

Close to the fort you can visit the remains of this important 17th century trading and pearl fishing town. Because of its power and wealth it attracted several invasions from Bahrain in the 18th century. Two areas have been reconstructed (the north house and the south house), and two further areas have been excavated – a souk area and a metal workers' shop. You can see the 11 hectare site clearly from the roof of Al Zubara fort; just turn left at the fort and take any of the tracks leading from the right hand side of the road.

The Inland Sea (Khor Al Adaid)
South-east Qatar

Khor Al Adaid, better known as the 'Inland Sea', is an area of outstanding natural beauty. It's about 60km south of Doha and can only be reached in a 4WD. It's also vital that you drive in convoy with at least one experienced off-road driver. The Inland Sea is an important area for resident and migratory bird species, such as flamingos, cormorants, waders, gulls and terns. Plans to make the Inland Sea a protected conservation area are under discussion.

Oryx Farm
Al Shahaniya, West of Doha

Located in the Al Shahaniya region in central Qatar, this protected farm houses a herd of Arabian oryx, which were once on the brink of extinction. The oryx is the national animal of Qatar. To visit this farm independently you need a special permit from the Ministry of Municipal Affairs and Agriculture, so it may be easier to go with a tour company.

Umm Salal Mohammed Fort
Umm Salal, North of Doha

This fort, built during the late 19th and early 20th centuries, sits about 20km north of Doha. It is notable for its thick high walls and impressive facade. Its 'T' shape is considered a unique architectural style in the Gulf. At the moment it is not open to the public. To get there take the North Road (Al Shamal Road) and follow the signpost to Umm Salal (sometimes Umm Slal).

Arabian oryx relaxing in the shade

Tours & Sightseeing

Forget huge buses – tours through Qatar are an intimate affair and offer an efficient and educational way to see the country and capital.

Most of the tour companies offer similar packages of trips in and around Doha. The absolute must-do is an excursion to the desert and the Inland Sea, camping overnight if you can. Several companies have permanent Arabic tents pitched there in the cooler months and offer some exhilarating dune bashing, after which they will cook a barbecue dinner and bring out the shisha.

Because the tour companies are fairly small local operations they can be very flexible in arranging whatever you want to do. Remember, the bigger your party the cheaper it will be. Below are some of the most common tours, followed by a list of the best tour operators in the country.

Boat Tours

Day or evening dhow cruises that either sail around Doha Bay or venture further afield to one of the small islands are very relaxing and give you the chance to see Doha from a whole new perspective. A traditional meal is provided and there may be music and entertainment too. The trips usually last around three or four hours. Boats leave from the dhow harbour off the Corniche. There are various options depending on how long you want to go for and how many people are in your group.

Regatta Sailing Academy
West Bay

550 7846
www.regattasailingacademy.com

The Regatta Sailing Academy has a range of sailing vessels to suit all requirements, including funboats, training boats, dinghies, and even a 28 foot yacht that can be used for pleasure or racing. The academy is staffed by fully qualified British Royal Yacht Academy instructors, who provide instruction in the safety of the lagoon area before venturing out into the waters of Doha Bay. Call for more information on prices and weather conditions. Map 2 E2

City Tours

If you are in Doha on a short visit or you want a crash course in finding your way around, then book a city tour of Doha. You will spend the day in an air-conditioned bus, with commentary provided by an English-speaking tour guide. The tours tend to cover the majority of the attractions listed in this book, including an in-depth tour of Souq Waqif (p.130).

Places Of Worship

Throughout the country there are several small mosques that are used by local Muslims. Non-Muslims are not necessarily forbidden from entering the mosques (although some, such as the Grand Mosque on Al Rayyan Road, are totally off limits), but it is unusual and there are no organised tours. To respect the Islamic faith, it may be better to appreciate the beauty of Qatar's mosques from the outside. If you do happen to gain access to the inside of a mosque remember to dress conservatively.

Country Tours

Several companies offer trips out of Doha. The Inland Sea is the most popular destination for a day trip or a night's camping in an Arab tent. Several companies, like Gulf Adventures, do a trip north of Doha which takes in Al Khor with its Corniche and dhow harbour, as well as forts, mangroves and an old sheikh's palace. Gulf Adventures also offer a tour to Shahaniya which includes the Sheikh Faisal Museum and Camel Racing Track. It can organise a group tour to Zekreet too, but the terrain is quite rough and there is a limit to where you can set up camp.

Safari Tours

A desert safari is a must-do in Qatar. You will be picked up in a powerful 4WD to head into the dunes for some thrilling off-road driving and spectacular scenery. Seatbelts are compulsory and, as you defy gravity by skimming round the edge of enormous sand dunes, you will understand why.

Main Tour Operators

Arabian Adventures   436 1461
Al Asmakh St, Al Jasra   www.arabianadventureqatar.com
A good range of tours is offered by Arabian Adventures, taking explorers on safari adventures, city tours and fishing trips. Its 'heritage tour' takes in the oryx and camel farm, while a desert safari offers the chance to explore the sand dunes in 4WD vehicles led by experienced Qatari guides. Map 5 C2

Black Pearl

435 7333
Al Ikhaa St
www.qatar-bp.com

Providing all of the most common Qatar tours, Black Pearl specialises in desert safaris. The company offers several desert packages, including buggy drives and opulent overnight trips. They also offer trips to the Inland Sea (p.90).

Gulf Adventures

422 1888
Al Amir St, Al Amir
www.gulf-adventures.com

Gulf Adventures provides a range of tours including an Inland Sea safari, complete with a Bedouin campsite on the beach. They also offer a four-day trip that explores the old towns and forts in the region. Keen divers can embark on the 'dive and drive' tour which takes in some of Qatar's best diving spots. Map 4 C3

Qatar International Adventures

455 3954
Al Hail Center, Old Airport Rd
www.qia-qatar.com

This is one of the few companies that organises trips to camel racetracks. If you really want to catch a race, be sure to confirm times from the company before booking. The company also offers most of the common tours, including city tours, desert safaris and shopping tours. Map 4 E3

Qatar International Tours

455 1141
Al Hail Center
www.qittour.com

This operator focuses on culturally themed tours. Choose to stay in the city and learn about its history up close, or cruise out to the desert to experience the Bedouin way of life. QIT also provides desert safaris and overnight packages. Map 4 E3

Sports & Spas

98 Active Qatar
112 Spectator Sports
120 Spas

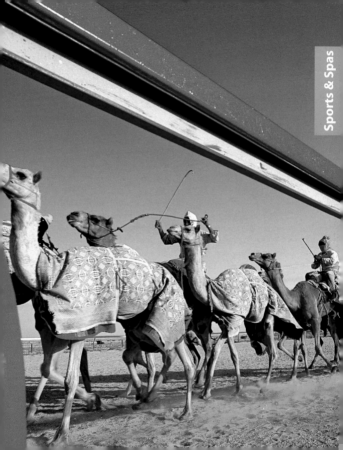

Active Qatar

Take advantage of the warm weather, fabulous beaches and varied landscape for dune bashing and watersports, or unwind at Qatar's luxurious spas.

With the exception of a short period in July and August when it becomes very humid, Qatar's location is an ideal one for participating in outdoor activities. You can also have a go at a variety of watersports; if you have always fancied trying a water-based activity, Qatar is the place to take it up. The great weather and warm sea should help tempt you into jumping on to a wakeboard, parasail or jet ski. There are also several good companies that offer diving and sailing trips for varying fees; costs will often include equipment hire and any training needed to participate.

If you prefer to be on dry land, a few tour operators offer desert safaris and dune-bashing tours, which can include overnight camping; this is a great way to get your adrenaline flowing while taking advantage of the region's spectacular landscape.

As befits a country that hosted the Asian Games in 2006, and is actively competing to stage the Fifa World Cup in 2018, Qatar has developed first-class facilities to generate sports-related tourism in the region. As a result, football, tennis and motorsports enthusiasts can take part in many sports and watch live action in state-of-the-art facilities. The Aspire Academy is Qatar's renowned sporting institute,

Al Sadd Sports Club

featuring an Olympic-sized pool, 200 metre athletics track and tennis courts.

If you are looking for ways to indulge, Qatar's luxurious spas and health clubs are largely based inside hotels and clubs, and many of these provide a range of exclusive treatments and services in elegant surroundings. You should find you have plenty of ways to pamper yourself in style, but those seeking more down-to-earth options won't be too hard pressed to find something more cost effective.

Camel Rides

Sealine Beach Resort

Mesaieed

476 5299
www.qnhc.com

This is your chance to experience something that you probably wouldn't get to do in your home country: a camel ride along the beach. It costs QR 15 for a quick ride, and QR 100 for an hour (padded shorts are recommended for this option). You will however be restricted to the resort boundaries.

Camping

Qatar International Tours

Various Locations

455 1141
www.qittour.com

Qatar International Tours provides all the camping equipment for tours including a fully furnished tent and water for the showers. A typical night starts with the lighting of a huge bonfire, and then a chef prepares a sumptuous barbecue feast. A minimum of eight people are required. A band and belly dancer are available on request (for an extra charge).

Dhow Charters

You can find dhows to rent in Navigation Dhow Harbour (in front of the Day Palace on the Corniche). There are a large number of tourist dhows of various sizes for rent, some with catering facilities. Phone numbers are usually displayed on the boats. Look at the smaller, less expensive dhows where the road turns into a T junction.

The Bay Club
West Bay, InterContinental Doha   484 4852   www.ichotelsgroup.com

You can charter a dhow for QR 75 per person, including lunch. The trip takes you to the nearby islands, or if you prefer you can just cruise along the Corniche. Trips can last anywhere between three and eight hours, depending on your preference (the price will vary accordingly). Map 2 E2

Palm Tree Island Boat Company
The Corniche,
  Next to Sheraton, West Bay   486 9151   alaaelshazly@hotmail.com

Palm Tree was recently remodelled as a smaller island and most facilities and features were removed, including the palm trees. Despite this, the Palm Tree Island Boat Company conducts pleasant dhow trips around the island for a reasonable QR 20 for adults and QR 15 for children; this includes a soft drink and snack. No booking is required.
Map 3 E3

Diving

Doha Sub Aqua Club
583 6240

DSAC Club House
 Ras Abu Abboud

www.dohasubaquaclub.com

DSAC offers a range of diving courses and awards BSAC qualifications. Shore dives are arranged to two artificial reefs that are still under construction. There are many wreck dives to be found. Trips to dive sites at Dukhan, Al Khor and the natural coral reefs in the Inland Sea are also organised. Map 4 F2

Pearl Divers
444 9553

Al Mirqab, Al Jadeed St, Al Mirqab Al Jadeed

Pearl Divers is a five-star PADI facility – its instructors can help you become a proficient diver in less than a week. After you've completed your training you will get the PADI open water diver certification, which is internationally recognised. Visit the Pearl Divers shop for a comprehensive range of diving equipment. Map 4 C2

Q-Dive Marine Center
437 5065

Souk Al Najada, Al Jasra

www.qdive.net

This centre offers a full range of diving services and equipment rental. It arranges diving, snorkelling and fishing trips, either with a speedboat or on a classic dhow. It also offers a range of diving courses accredited under PADI. Map 5 D3

Fishing

The clear, warm waters of the Arabian Gulf provide rich fishing grounds. During the fishing season (October to May) you should be able to enjoy some successful trips where your haul could include kingfish, tuna, mackerel, and barracuda. The water frontage of the Corniche also provides an ideal spot. Alternatively, you can take part in an organised dhow trip through a tour company. If you wish to organise your own group, most of the dhows are berthed in Navigation Harbour on the Corniche (contact details will be on the vessel).

Qatar International Tours
455 1141

Various Locations
www.qittour.com

Qatar International Tours has a full range of options. A full-day fishing trip costs QR 180 on a traditional dhow, or QR 200 on the fishing boat. The price includes fishing line, bait, lunch and soft drinks. The captain is highly experienced and guides the boat to locations that will yield the best catch.

Golf

Doha Golf Club
496 0777

New District of Doha 69
www.dohagolfclub.com

Doha Golf Club is open daily to all. It has a 7,312 yard, 18 hole Championship course and a floodlit nine-hole Academy course. It is also home to several restaurants, lounges and conference rooms. The club also hosts the Qatar Masters tournament. Map 2 D1

Horse Riding

Qatar Racing & Equestrian Club   480 6011
Al Rayyan Farm, Al Rayyan

Qatar Racing & Equestrian Club offers riding tuition for
all ages, conducted by qualified instructors. You'll need to
complete an application form and pay monthly subscription
fees (QR 300), which entitles you to three lessons per week.
A certificate confirming medical fitness to ride is required.
Map 1 B3

Sealine Beach Resort   476 5299
Mesaieed   www.qnhc.com

At this resort you can enjoy a horse ride along the beach
for QR 15. Camel rides are also available (although you'll be
taken around on a lead). If you can ride you can hire a horse
unaccompanied for one hour for QR 100. However you will be
restricted to the resort boundaries.

Kayaking

Sealine Beach Resort   476 5299
Mesaieed   www.qnhc.com

This resort is a haven for water fanatics as it offers many
watersports from its beautiful stretch of private beach,
including pedal boating, jet skiing and aqua cycles. You can
hire a kayak for QR 40 per hour. You will be constrained to the
resort for safety reasons. Life jackets are provided.

Top: Qatar Racing & Equestrian Club. Bottom: Doha Golf Club

Kitesurfing

Qatar Kite Surfing Club
535 0336

Various Locations   qatarkitesurfing@hotmail.com

One of the fastest growing and most exciting watersports is kitesurfing. The main venues are the shallow waters of Zekrit Bay on the west coast and the similarly sheltered and shallow waters off West Bay in Doha. Qatar Kite Surfing Club organises activities for those interested in learning the sport or perfecting their skills.

Parasailing

Diplomatic Club
484 7444

West Bay Lagoon   www.thediplomaticclub.com

Among other watersports and activities available at the Diplomatic Club, you can have a go at parasailing. Increasingly popular but not one for the faint-hearted, parasailing involves being strapped into a parachute that is pulled along the coast by speedboat. One session costs QR 100 for adults and QR 75 for children. Map 2 E1

Sheraton Doha Resort & Convention Hotel
485 4444

Corniche St, West Bay   www.starwoodhotels.com

A parasailing session here lasts for about 15 minutes, which is plenty of time to take in the beautiful coastline as you hover over the clear waters. Due to the popularity, it is necessary to book in advance; a session costs QR 100. Map 4 F3

Powerboating

Diplomatic Club
484 7444

West Bay Lagoon · www.thediplomaticclub.com

The Diplomatic Club has a 21 foot powerboat that can be hired for daytrips, fishing trips, waterskiing and island drop-offs. The hire includes an experienced captain. If you are waterskiing, instruction is available, and safety cover is provided by trained lifeguards on jet skis. Map 2 E1

Quad Bikes

Sealine Beach Resort
476 5299

Mesaieed · www.qnhc.com

As long as you are 16 years old and have a valid driving licence (for identification purposes), you can hire a quad bike from the Sealine Beach Resort. It costs QR 150 per hour for a big quad bike (160cc) and QR 100 per hour for the medium or small quad bike (80cc or 50cc). Helpful attendants will show you how to operate the vehicles and assist you if you get stuck in the sand.

Sailing

Qatar Sailing & Rowing Federation
443 9840

Ras Abu Abboud Rd, Al Khulaifat · www.qatarsailing.org

The Qatar Sailing & Rowing Federation is responsible for promoting sailing in the country, with the support of the Doha Sailing Club. The club has a variety of boats suitable for all ages. Racing takes place at 13:00 every Friday and regattas are organised regularly. Introductory lessons for beginners are given every Saturday (wind strength permitting) and a try-sail will cost no more than a phone call to the club. Map 4 F2

Regatta Sailing Academy   550 7846

InterContinental Doha,
 West Bay   www.regattasailingacademy.com

The academy has a range of equipment suitable for all ages, including lasers, catamarans and sports boats. You can seek the advice of fully qualified British Royal Yacht Association instructors, and get some pointers in the safety of the lagoon before progressing to the waters of Doha Bay. Map 2 E2

Sand Boarding

For thrills and spills, desert style, try sand boarding on the dunes. You won't reach the breakneck speeds of snow boarding, and if you do fall off you land in lovely soft sand. This must-try activity is offered by most of the tour operators.

Blokart Paradise   507 2661

Nr Mesaieed

Blokarting, a land sport that has much in common with watersports, has recently been organised in Qatar, with a regular venue near Mesaieed. Suitable for both experienced karters and beginners, Blokarting is ideally suited to the hard desert areas of Qatar. It is best to call ahead first as it is located in a remote area, off the beaten track, and it can be difficult to find.

Qatar International Tours
Various Locations

455 1141
www.qittour.com

Whether you choose to go on the half-day or full-day desert safari with Qatar International Tours, you'll have the opportunity to try sand skiing. A half-day tour lasts four hours and costs QR 200 per person. A full-day tour costs QR 275 and lasts eight hours. Four participants are required for each tour.

Snorkelling

Q-Dive Marine Center
Souk Al Najada, Al Jasra

437 5065
www.qdive.net

Apart from being a top-class dive centre Q-Dive also offers snorkelling trips. Its fully-trained staff are on hand for those who are new to snorkelling and Q-Dive will also arrange equipment hire. Depending on the weather, there are weekly trips to either the southern or northern waters off Qatar's coast. Day trips are available to the Banana and Safliya Islands.
Map 5 D3

Wadi & Dune Bashing

Qatar boasts some impressive sand dunes, reaching heights of nearly 50 metres. With a skilled driver behind the wheel, you can spend a thrilling afternoon racing up sand dunes and navigating your way down the other side. Unless you are extremely experienced, it is safer to enlist the help of one of the tour operators than to attempt dune bashing yourself. If you do go off into the desert in your own vehicle, always adhere to safety precautions and, most importantly, travel in convoy.

Gulf Adventures
422 1888

Al Amir St, Al Amir · www.gulf-adventures.com

Gulf Adventures' comprehensive range of tours includes desert safaris and camping trips. For the ultimate desert safari, take the overnight desert tour, which includes a stay in a Bedouin campsite after you've spent the day dune bashing (QR 550 per person). A dune discovery day tour is also offered daily for QR 240 per person. Map 4 A3

Qatar International Tours
455 1141

Various Locations · www.qittour.com

Experience the thrill of riding up and over dunes and through rugged wadis on an organised trip with Qatar International Tours. You can choose from a half-day tour (four hours at QR 200 per person) or a full-day tour (which lasts eight hours and costs QR 275 each). There must be a minimum of four participants per trip.

Wakeboarding

Diplomatic Club
484 7444

West Bay Lagoon · www.thediplomaticclub.com

A range of watersports is available here, and non-members can pay an entry fee to use the facilities (QR 75 on weekdays, QR 100 at weekends). Wakeboarding is available for adults and children. It costs QR 100 per hour and there is no extra charge for instruction. All watersports are available from 09:00 to just before sunset. Map 2 E1

Powerboats on the Corniche

Waterskiing

Diplomatic Club

West Bay Lagoon

484 7444

www.thediplomaticclub.com

The Diplomatic Club has a 21 foot powerboat that can be hired for waterskiing, or for day excursions and fishing trips. Instructors are on hand if you need lessons, and there are trained lifeguards ready to come to the rescue (on their own jetski's) should you need assistance. An hour session of waterskiing costs QR 100, with no extra charge for coaching.

Map 2 E1

Spectator Sports

Qatar features some of the finest sports stadiums in the world, part of a strategy to develop the nation into a regional hub for sports-related tourism.

As part of government plans to develop and promote Qatar's appeal for sports-related tourism, the Aspire Academy centre of excellence has been established in Doha. Here any national who shows ability in a particular sport will be developed according to programmes set up by top-class trainers and coaches. Athletes gain experience in their discipline through international events organised by Aspire, and the venue features first-rate competition areas and spectator facilities.

Depending on schedules, you may be able to see some of the world's top high divers or gymnasts in action, free of charge, alongside other minority sports. However, these events are often poorly publicised and the only way to find out what is going on is to keep a close eye on the local press.

As in the majority of countries, the dominant sport is football, with motorsports coming second in popularity. The premium facilities for watching football here are very good, and are comparable with some of the sport's top stadia. Other sports have not been neglected though: billions of riyals have been spent on spectator facilities, particularly in the case of tennis, badminton, and motorsports.

Regular sporting events are not guaranteed to take place at a specific time each year, although some events, such as major tennis internationals, can usually be pinned down to within

Aspire Academy sports complex

a month. Timing is often further complicated by the fact that the holy month of Ramadan usually arrives 12 days earlier each year. Major sporting fixtures are often rescheduled to avoid this period.

Camel Racing

Camel racing is big in Qatar. The centre of the sport is Shahaniyah, which is about 20 kilometres west of Doha, on the road to Dukhan. Here there are a collection of camel breeding farms and studs, complete with a 10 kilometre camel-racing track and grandstand (Qatar Camel Racing Committee, Shahaniyah Race Track, 487 2028).

You can watch a race from the stands or, for a more thrilling experience, join the owners who use the outer track to follow their animals around in an attempt to encourage them to win. The latter option is an exciting experience, but don't get too close, as driving standards are a little worrying.

Cycling

The international highlight of this sport is the gruelling Tour de France, but the best competitors also regularly participate in the Tour of Qatar. While flatter and smaller than France, Qatar is certainly much hotter, even in the cooler months of January or February when the event is usually scheduled. Roads are closed while the race is taking place and all you have to do is turn up (the local press will announce the venue). The competition always ends at the Corniche. The Tour de France website (www.letour.fr) has information on the Qatar event, including course maps.

Equestrian Sports

Horse racing happens in Qatar throughout the winter months at the impressive Qatar Racing & Equestrian Club (p.104). Other forms of equestrian sport are catered for in Qatar, including an Arabian horse show in March, also held at the Qatar Racing & Equestrian Club (the local press will provide the exact timings of the event). The Desert Marathon takes place during the relatively cooler winter months south of Mesaieed. A course is laid in the valleys between the sand dunes, and riders from around the world compete in the event. To watch this sport all you need is a four-wheel drive vehicle and a picnic. Just sit in the desert and wait for the riders to pass by. Keep an eye on the local press for timings.

Qatar Racing & Equestrian Club   480 6011
www.qrec.gov.qa   Al Rayyan Farm, Al Rayyan
Races are scheduled every Thursday from about 16:00 until about 21:00 entry is completely free of charge. Although gambling is prohibited, race-goers can put their names into free raffles based on what they think the winning horse will be. Prizes are substantial, and often include cars. The course is also floodlit, with good coverage on huge TV screens. Map 1 B3

Football

There is no spectator sport in Qatar bigger than football. Domestic competition consists of 18 teams, which are formed into two leagues (see the Qatar Football Association website for information on teams.) The season runs through the cooler months from October to April. International matches and friendly tours are usually played at the stadiums belonging to the larger Q-League teams, such as Al-Arabi, Al-Sadd, and Rayyan. Football fans from overseas can watch a game for a meagre amount, ranging from free to QR 10 if it happens to be an international match.

Football violence is unheard of – but when a major match is won, fans tend to leap into their four-wheel drives and drive up and down Doha Corniche with revellers standing on car roofs, revving their engines and burning up their tyres; it is not malicious, but it is best avoided.

Golf

In January each year the Doha Golf Club (483 2338, www. dohagolfclub.com) in West Bay hosts the Qatar Masters PGA Championship tournament (495 0731, www.qatar-masters. com) on its pleasant course, designed by Peter Harradine. The event, like many in the region, offers major prize money and attracts some of the best players from around the world.

It is not unknown for local golf aficionados to spend part of their annual leave watching the Masters – it is an opportunity to watch the best golf at close quarters without the usual hindrance of crowds. The governing body is the Qatar Golf Association (483 7815, www.qga.com.qa).

Motorsports

Designed primarily as a motorcycle track, Losail hosts a round of the Superbike World Championship (www.worldsbk.com), which is normally held in February, and it is the setting for the Qatar heat of the MotoGP (www.motogp.com), usually staged in March. Follow the new Al Khor road from Doha for about 10 kilometres and the purpose-built Losail racetrack, is signposted on your right. Spectators are restricted to the large stand on the fast starting and finishing straight, and visibility can be obscured by the pit buildings opposite. However, the stand does provide ample shade from the sun and a good view of the action in the pits.

The track is occasionally used for car racing, and rounds of the Grand Prix Masters series (www.themastersseries.com) have been held here. Entrance fees are low, but this depends on the status of the event taking place.

Qatar International Rally
Various Locations

437 9884
www.qmmf.com

The highlight of motor rallying is the Qatar International Rally. This event takes place over three days in January. The location of the rally sites, which take full advantage of the country's desert terrain, varies from year to year and you will need to keep an eye on the local press for more information on its location.

Qatar Motor & Motorcycle Federation
Salwa Rd, Al Muntazah

437 9884
www.qmmf.com

Qatar Motor & Motorcycle Federation is the governing body for motorsports in Qatar, and holds several car and motorcycle rallies throughout the year. The federation is always on the lookout for keen volunteers who can help with the events. Visit the website to download a volunteer application form. Map 5 A4

Powerboat Racing

This is a popular sport in Qatar, run under the umbrella of the Qatar Marine Sports Federation (QMSF), which organises world-class events in powerboat racing and equips local sportsmen to take part in international competitions. There are no membership fees but registration fees are required to take part in the events. The leading powerboat sports here are Class 1 Offshore Powerboat Racing and Formula 2000 Powerboat Racing (Boat GP). Every year the QMSF organises two rounds of Class 1 Offshore Powerboat Racing, one round of Formula 2000 Powerboat Racing and one round of the Middle East Formula 2000 Powerboat Championships. For more information visit the QMSF website, www.qmsf.org, or call 437 9744.

Squash

The Qatar Classic Squash Championship (www.qatarsquash. com) usually attracts the cream of the world's players to the Khalifa Tennis Complex (440 9666), but the timing of the event seems to be variable (check the website for updates.) Spectator facilities for events are good and attending a game will not break the bank. Unusually for Qatar, the competitions for men and women occur at the same time. When the tournaments are over, the players move on with their prize money and things return to normal – which means you can then play both tennis and squash on the very same courts as the professionals. The Qatar Squash Federation (488 7671) oversees the game at a national level.

Khalifa Tennis Stadium

Tennis

You can see the biggest tennis stars here for a negligible price and, unless it is a final match, you will have the pick of the seats. Men compete in the annual Qatar ExxonMobil Open (www.qatartennis.org) which takes place in late December or early January. Prize money is substantial and consequently all the best players turn up. The women's equivalent, the Qatar Total Open (www.qatartennis.org), commences a month after the men's competition. Matches for both take place in Khalifa Tennis Complex (440 9666). For more information on the tournaments see the website of the Qatar Tennis Federation (www.qatartennis.org) or call 483 2991.

Spas

Relax and recharge at one of Doha's luxury hotel spas, which offer a multitude of pampering treatments and several ways for you to unwind.

Health Spas

Bio-Bil Health, Beauty Centre & Spa   493 4433

Bilal Suites, Diplomatic District   biobil@qatar.com.qa

Bio-Bil offers head-to-toe pampering in luxurious surroundings. Options include aromatherapy facials, treatments for wrinkles or sun spots, body scrubs and massages. After your treatment you can use the swimming pool and other facilities such as steam room, spa bath, and relaxation room. Monthly and yearly memberships are available. Map 3 D2

The Spa   429 8520

Marriott Doha, Al Khulaifat   www.marriotthotels.com

This spa offers treatments to pamper every inch of your body, from therapeutic back massages and Turkish baths to scrubs and facial treatments. Other treatments include body wraps, fitness counselling, foot baths, manicures, pedicures, therapy baths and waxing. Map 4 F2

The Spa, Ritz-Carlton Doha   484 8173

West Bay Lagoon   www.ritzcarlton.com

Offering complete luxury for men and women, this spa provides seven private treatment rooms, as well as a sauna, a steam room, an indoor pool and roman baths. Treatments include Oriental massage and hydrotherapy. There are separate facilities for men and women. The spa also offers a range of day and overnight packages (check the website for more details). Map 2 E3

Six Senses Spa at Sharq Village & Spa
Al Khulaifat

425 6999
www.sixsenses.com/six-senses-spas

This impressive spa has 23 treatment rooms to choose from, together with an impressive menu. The spa is traditionally decorated, in luxurious surroundings, with plunge pools, saunas, and relaxation rooms. A wide range of facial and body treatments are available here, including Balinese, Swedish, and aromatherapy. The spa offers a number of packages to suit all needs, with the inclusion of relaxing classes such as tai chi and meditation. Check the website for further information. Map 4 F2

Spa & Wellness Centre
Four Seasons Hotel,
Diplomatic District

494 8888

www.fourseasons.com/doha

The unique facilities in this state-of-the-art spa include a hydrotherapy lounge and pool, cool and warm plunge pools, a reflexology foot bath, heated laconium beds, a colour therapy room, and a meditation room. Other treatments offered include wraps, scrubs and Thai massage. There are separate areas for men and women, and you can also hire your own private spa suite complete with a whirlpool. Complimentary refreshments are offered in the relaxation areas. Map 3 F2

Shopping

124 Shopping In Qatar

126 Hotspots

128 Markets & Souks

134 Shopping Malls

138 Department Stores

140 Where To Go For...

Shopping In Qatar

Whether you decide to splurge in luxurious malls or wander around authentic souks, Qatar has something for everyone.

The shopping scene in Qatar has developed a great deal over the years – as the population has expanded, so has the retail potential. Many international brands and retailers have taken the opportunity to move into a new and growing market. From high-end brand name boutiques right down to funky little one-man stores in the souks, traditional and modern blend together to bring surprises and bargains. Qatar should keep most shopaholics happily swiping their credit cards. Big shopping centres all house major international brands, and because there is no sales tax or VAT you might find some things cheaper than in your home country, but this is not always the case.

While new shopping centres are in the pipeline, the big three – Villaggio Mall (p.135), City Center Doha (p.134) and Landmark Shopping Mall (p.134) – can service just about every shopping need you have, and then some. Many of the larger malls feature big department stores (p.138) that sell a good range of cosmetics, clothing and jewellery.

Malls are not concentrated in one area of Doha in particular; you'll find them scattered around, which can be something of a hassle given the growing traffic problem in the city and the extensive road building operations. But with plentiful parking and reasonably priced taxis, mall hopping can be relatively drama free.

Each summer, usually from 1 July, Doha hosts the Shopping Festival (p.36). This is when prices are reduced in most stores by up to 50%. Ramadan is also a good period to snare a bargain, as many stores drop their prices or have special offers.

The traditional markets (souks, see p.129) are a must. Many are clustered together near the Souk Waqif (p.130) area so you can wander from one to the other quite easily. Souk Waqif is a landmark in Doha and one of the most beautiful in the Middle East. There is a huge range of shops and the choices are growing. It's not just a shopping destination – dozens of great eateries are opening in the area as well, and there are traditional dance performances and other entertainment during the cooler months.

Souks are particularly enjoyable for shoppers who like to rummage, and there are unbelievable bargains to be had if you've got the time to look.

Shops Outside Doha
Shopping outside of Doha is less appealing than in the capital; luxury malls and interesting souks are few and far between, although new and growing communities in Al Khor (p.5) and Al Wakrah (p.5) signal a future change. If you can't find what you're looking for in Doha, chances are you won't find it in the surrounding area either, so a trip to nearby Dubai or Abu Dhabi might be the answer.

Hotspots

For a shopping experience beyond the malls, try exploring the eclectic mix of stores and markets near Salwa Road.

In general, malls are the most popular areas to shop; not just because of the variety of well-known stores, but also because in summer they are cool thanks to powerful air-conditioning.

There are a few other places where you can get some retail therapy. **Salwa Road** (Map 4 D3) is home to various independent outlets that are visited frequently by all kinds of shoppers. You'll find Jarir Bookstore (444 0212), Apollo Furniture (468 9522) and Skate Shack (469 2532), to name just a few. Salwa Road is famous for its many furniture shops, although most of the stock is for those with rather flamboyant tastes. One of the nice things about shopping on Salwa Road is the availability of parking spaces.

Al Mirqab Street (Map 4 C2) is another popular shopping destination. It has several fabric shops and tailors, a great art shop, stores where you can get upholstery or have curtains made, phone shops, toy shops and a few pharmacies.

Al Sadd Street (Map 4 C2) also has a number of interesting shops, as well as the newly opened Royal Plaza shopping centre (p.137).

The souk areas are popular and offer a vibrant glimpse into traditional life. The food and fabric souks are popular with all nationalities. The **Musheirib** (Map 4 C2) area (better known as the Sofitel shopping complex) has numerous

Window shopping

shops selling everything from cheap fabric to top-of-the-range TVs. It is very busy at weekends though, and the parking situation is a nightmare.

Despite the bustling activity of the souks, many people choose to go to shopping malls, especially in the summer, simply because everything is under one roof. There is no doubt that souks should be on the list of things to do with visitors from out of town.

The **Central Market** (Map 4 B4) area along Salwa Road is where you will find the food and livestock markets. This area is well worth a visit every now and then to stock up on fruit, vegetables and fresh fish.

Markets & Souks

Pick up anything from stuffed camels to traditional spices in Doha's souks; these bustling markets offer a chance to experience a fragment of local life.

The souks in Doha sell a huge range of items. Much of what you can buy in the souks can also be found in shopping centres and supermarkets but, as a general rule, souks tend to be cheaper because you have the power of bargaining.

On the whole, these bustling markets are fascinating not only from a shopper's point of view (you could spend an entire morning rummaging around), but also because of the cultural experience – it is a good chance to get up close and personal with a traditional form of business.

Bargaining is a skill that should be practised and enjoyed. Vendors are friendly and eager to make a sale, and they expect a bit of negotiating from their customers. Shop around first so that you know what something is worth, and use that as a starting point for your negotiations.

Remember that souks are traditional areas often predominately populated by men, so it's wise for women to dress conservatively, with shoulders and legs covered. If you wear something tight or revealing then be prepared to be gawked at.

Souk Waqif (the Old Souk) is an extraordinary place, where you can buy a traditional Qatari outfit then walk up the street to eat at a Moroccan restaurant (see Tajine, p.200) before picking up some kitchen appliances on your way home. Outside of Souk Waqif, all of Doha's main souks (the Omani Market, Fruit and Vegetable Market, Fish Market and Animal Market) are situated in the same area south-west of the city on Salwa Road.

Omani Market

Salwa Rd, Al Maamoura

The Omani Market sells plants, pots, garden materials and a selection of woven mats and baskets, which are imported from Oman and, increasingly, Iran and India. There are also a few stalls selling nuts and dates. There isn't a huge choice of pots, but it is worth taking the time to browse through all the plants. Don't forget to bargain with the friendly and enthusiastic vendors for a better price. There are a number of plant nurseries in the surrounding area selling pots and plants. Map 4 B4

Thursday & Friday Market

Salwa Rd, Al Maamoura

Located opposite the Fish Market, this market is only operational on two days of the week, in the evenings. In its heyday, it was one of the busiest markets in the city. But sadly, after a fire two years ago, it is now a shadow of its former self. Vendors sell assorted goods such as perfume, clothes, carpets, fabric and household items. There are a few permanent shops in the area selling similar items, but the selection is poor compared with what you will find in the market. Map 4 B4

Souk Waqif

Souk Waqif, Al Jasra   www.soukwaqif.com

With its cobblestone labyrinth of alleyways, mud walls and wooden beams, it's hard to believe this impressive version of Souk Waqif is just a few years old. The souk's history dates back to when Doha was a tiny village divided by Wadi Mishireb. The actual site of Souk Waqif (or to taxi drivers the 'old souk') sits between Al Souk Street and Grand Hamad Street. The area had been run down until the government restored it to its original glory in 2004.

The souk's open-air area hosts cultural activities, entertainment and dining. Locals and residents alike head here for items ranging from cooking pots to traditional dress. The souk is known for its spice market, offering pungent delicacies from around the Gulf, Middle East and Asia. Other offerings include honey from Yemen, pashminas from Kashmir and 'antiques' from India. Along the central outdoor area you can find men weaving traditional Bedouin blankets and cushion covers for majlis style furniture. The area also includes the Waqif Art Center (p.82). Further buildings surrounding the main souk are being renovated, to be completed in 2010. Most stalls open in the morning but it's livelier after 16:00. Map 5 C2

Around Souk Waqif

Gold Souk

With gold reaching record prices around the globe, it remains a bargain commodity in this part of the world. Many expats

prefer to take gold rather than cash back to their home country. The government regulates the purity of gold, so you can be assured it's all great quality. The gold on display here ranges from the spectacular Indian and Arab bridal jewellery through to humble bracelets, all in 18 carat or 22 carat. The Gold Souk can be found just off Ali Bin Abdullah Street.

Souk Al Ahmed, Souk Al Dira & Souk Al Asiery

These three souks are great stops for those who wish to recreate the latest catwalk look or design their own creations. Souk Al Ahmed, also known as the 'bridal souk', is an air-conditioned two storey building off Grand Hamed Street that houses dozens of specialist bridal tailors. Souk Al Dira, which is also known as the 'button and bow souk', is the place to buy fabric by the metre. You'll find a good range of material here from simple cotton right through to the finest silk. Stores in this souk also sell all manner of accoutrements to ensure you have everything you need to make a one-of-a-kind creation. Souk Al Asiery is a cheaper version of souks Al Ahmed and Al Dira, which are all located on Al Ahmed Street. Souk Al Asiery is the place to go to find all kinds of fabrics at knockdown prices.

Souk Al Jabor

You will find everything from perfume, toys, and cheap shoes to tacky souvenirs in this jumble of a souk. Located on Al Ahmed Street, you will need to take your patience with you and be prepared to spend some time rummaging around to find the things you need.

Souk Waqif

Souk Haraj

This quiet little gem on Al Mansoura Street is as close as Doha gets to a flea market. Shops here sell locally made furniture at great prices. The carpentry and metalwork stores located just off the main square also sell curtains, carpets and assorted items of furniture. The majority of the furniture is imported from India and Pakistan, and business is conducted off the back of trucks and trailers. You can also pick up second-hand crockery, jewellery and tools.

Souk Nasser Bin Saif

This is the electronics souk, where you can find everything a new home requires. CDs, DVDs and even the odd audio tape are on sale here.

Shopping Malls

When the heat is on Qataris head indoors, and the luxurious air-conditioned malls filled with high fashion are a perfect refuge.

City Center Doha   483 9990
Diplomatic District

You could spend an entire day in City Center and still not get to experience everything it has to offer. The centre features outlets selling a variety of international and local merchandise. Numerous cafes are scattered throughout the mall, as well as a broad range of food outlets.

There are also plenty of ways to entertain kids including an ice rink, ten-pin bowling alley and a children's entertainment centre. There is also a spa and a salon (exclusively for ladies), a gym and a 14 screen cinema. Despite the massive carpark, finding a spot at the weekends can be a chore. City Center is open from 10:00 to 22:00 Saturday to Thursday, and from 14:00 to 22:00 on Fridays. Carrefour opens at 08:00 every day.
Map 3 D2

Landmark Shopping Mall   487 5222
Madinat Khalifa, North   www.landmarkdoha.com

This mall is in the style of a Qatari castle. Inside you'll find a variety of international and local stores, renowned brands and the latest worldwide fashion. The mall is also popular for its two large UK department stores Marks & Spencer and Bhs. The centre also has a foodcourt with typical fastfood outlets like McDonald's, Hardee's, Pizza Hut and Subway, but there are a few restaurants including TGI Friday's and Pizza Express. Landmark hosts a number of art exhibitions and events, and during special occasions and festivals (like Eid) there is plenty of family entertainment within the mall. Parking can be difficult at the weekend, but it's free. Most of the shops open at either 09:00 or 10:00 and close at 22:00. On Fridays, all shops open at 13:00. Map 2 B3

Villaggio Mall   413 5222
Al Aziziyah

Perhaps the most stylish mall in Doha, Villaggio Mall is located in the shadow of the Aspire Tower (p.75). As you pass through the doors you are transported to an Italian village by the sea, with gondola rides in the canal and the illusion of blue skies between villas and storefronts. Villaggio comes complete with cafes, family restaurants, an ice hockey rink, Carrefour, a Virgin Megastore, the largest Quiksilver in the region and many other brand names. The flagship store in the new extension is Louis Vuitton. There is free parking (some of it covered) around the mall. Carrefour opens at 08:00, Starbucks opens at 08:30 and the other shops open anywhere between 09:00 and 10:00. The mall closes at 22:00. Map 4 A3

Centrepoint   442 1766
Al Defal St, Nr Sports Roundabout, Al Sadd

Centrepoint, also called Al Samakh, is the little mall with big shops. Babyshop has children's toys for all ages, playhouses, cots, beds and clothing. Close by you'll find Splash, with very reasonably priced clothes, and Shoe Mart with a broad selection for children and adults. There are some fastfood places, but nothing like the range in the larger malls. The Home Centre has a good range of furniture and takes up a large portion of the top floor. Opposite Home Centre is a small children's play area called Fun City (p.55), which is a great distraction for bored kids and tired parents. There is also an optician where you can buy sunglasses, and a small electronics shop selling well known brand names. There is street and underground parking, which is well illuminated with easy access to the mall. Map 4 C2

Hyatt Plaza

Al Waab St, Al Aziziyah

469 4848
www.hyattplaza.com

You'll recognise Hyatt Plaza from the enormous shopping trolley in the carpark, which you can see from the roundabout by Khalifa Stadium. The trolley is an advert for Giant (469 2991), the excellent supermarket located in the centre. This mall is smaller than some of the other malls and it has a limited selection of shops, but the furniture shop Homes R Us is popular. There is a smattering of high-street brands including The Body Shop, Mothercare, and Paris Gallery. You can also get anything from ceramics to chopsticks at Daiso Japanese discount store (469 8999). There is also a large foodcourt with a fair selection of food outlets. If you have children to amuse, Jungle Zone, a mini version of a theme park, is a decent attempt to keep the little ones happy. Parking, especially at the weekend, can be challenging to say the least. Map 4 A3

The Mall
467 8888

D Ring Rd, Al Matar Al Qadeem

The Mall was the first shopping centre to open in Doha, in the mid 1990s. Since then it has grown into one of the most popular places for shopping and meeting friends. Radio Shack, Paul Frank, Birkenstock, Mont Blanc, Givenchy and Monsoon are among the outlets here. There is a three-screen cinema showing the latest American, European and Arabic films. A foodcourt houses typical treats and, if you like to be creative with your coffee, Café Ceramique, on the upper level, allows you to paint your own ceramic plates, cups and bowls while having a snack. The Mall is host to a number of exhibitions and special events throughout the year. It is very popular with families during festival time, when there is plenty of entertainment. Map 4 E3

Royal Plaza
413 0000

Al Sadd St, Al Sadd
www.royalplazadoha.com

This luxury mall offers a white glove service where you can pre-book a gentleman to assist with your shopping and carry all those bags. Small but perfectly formed, its three retail levels consist of boutiques such as Cartier, Mont Blanc, Levi's, Givenchy, Oilily and Morgan, to name a few. There are a variety of features available including a gift idea service, limousine services, baby changing facilities, complimentary strollers, lost and found, shoe polishing, mobile recharging and wheelchairs. The art deco-style Movie Palace opened in 2008 and is the plush place to catch the latest English, Arabic and Hindi releases. Map 4 C2

Department Stores

Department stores here may pale in comparison to the colossal shopping centres in Europe or America, but they are still good for one-stop shopping.

Blue Salon

446 6111
www.bluesalon.com

C Ring Rd, Ibn Mahmood South

Blue Salon is one of the premier department stores in Doha. It carries a range of brands including Armani, Valentino, Aigner and Diesel. The shop sells the typical products found in a department store, like linen, electronic goods and men's and women's fashion items. The ladies-only fashion section is laden with high-end brands. Map 4 D2

Highland

467 8678

The Mall, Al Matar Al Qadeem

Highland sells a variety of items including high-end cosmetics and perfumes, clothing and luggage. The children's section caters to younger kids. This eclectic store also has an interesting souvenir section where you buy a crystal falcon if your heart so desires it. Map 4 E3

Marks & Spencer

488 0101

Landmark Shopping Mall,
 Madinat Khalifa (North)
www.marksandspencerme.com

Those not familiar with Marks & Spencer are in for a treat – it is a great department store that is very popular with both expats and locals. The Doha branch is not as big as you might find in other countries, but the store has a great selection of fashion items for the whole family as well as a wide selection of men's suits. The children's clothes range from newborns right up to trendy teens. The ladies' section has a lovely range of the latest fashion and clothes are available in a wide range of sizes, from petite to plus-size. The underwear section is famous: you'll find garments for everyone, but the women's section is a haven of pretty colours and styles ranging from stylish to sensible. Map 2 B3

Merch

467 4314

The Mall, Al Matar Al Qadeem

Merch is another high-end department store, and its defining feature is its enviable cosmetic and perfume section which holds a variety of international brands. You can also pick up the usual range of handbags, accessories and male and female fashion items found in most other department stores. There is another branch of the store on Salwa Road (465 8656). Map 4 E3

Salam Plaza

483 2050

City Center Doha, Diplomatic District   www.salams.com

Salam is a well-known name in this part of the world: its department stores, Salam Plaza and Salam Studio (The Mall, p.137), carry a wide range of upmarket, good quality merchandise including clothing, cosmetics, perfumes, luggage, household goods and shoes. This is not the place for avid bargain hunters (except during the sales). Map 3 D2

Where To Go For...

Carpets

Most carpets sold in Qatar have been made in countries such as Iran, India, Pakistan or China. Persian carpets are regarded as being the best investment. The price of an original Persian carpet can reach tens of thousands of riyals. They are usually extremely attractive and they take years to make. Hand-made carpets are more valuable than machine-made ones, and silk is more expensive than wool. The more knots per square metre, the better the carpet.

The best places to buy carpets are the major shopping malls like City Center Doha and Royal Plaza. To make sure the carpet you are buying is original, ask for a certificate of authenticity. You can get cheaper carpets in the souks but be aware that shop owners are very convincing and will make you believe you are getting a great product at a low price.

Jewellery & Watches

There are numerous outlets selling watches and jewellery, many of which are in shopping malls. Most major watch brands are available and price tags range from under QR 100 to over QR 100,000.

Louis Vuitton at Villaggio is the newest player on the high-end watch pitch; the new boutique has a specialised 'watch salon' with exclusive and bespoke items on sale. You will also find plenty of watches on sale in the souks, including some pretty convincing imitations. Jewellery is sold by weight and you may find that prices are cheaper here compared to your home country. Every mall will have at least one jeweller, such as the ubiquitous Damas, and of course the Gold Souk is a wall-to-wall wonderland of glittering gold shops. The Gold Souk is located on Ali Bin Abdullah Street and the surrounding area.

If you don't see anything you like, it is easy to find a jeweller who will make an item to your specifications. Instances of jewellers conning their customers by selling fake gold at real-gold prices are few and far between; nevertheless it is a good idea to ask for a certificate of authenticity (especially important when buying diamonds). Many stores are clustered around Al Sadd Street as well as the souks, so shop around.

Souvenirs

Don't fall into the 'my grandma went to Doha and all I got was this lousy T-shirt' souvenir trap; Doha has a wide range of interesting mementos on offer that reflect the special character of Arabia. Souvenirs tend to be similar throughout the GCC countries. Intricately carved wooden trinket boxes, Arabian incense, shisha pipes, fluffy singing camels and miniature brass coffee pots have all found their way into many a suitcase on its way out of the GCC, and Doha is no exception. There are also numerous souvenirs made using sand, the region's most abundant resource, such as sand pictures and jars holding different coloured sand. Most hotels have little lobby shops that sell a limited range of the standard offerings, but for the best souvenir shopping in Doha head for the souks. Here you'll find wall-to-wall mementos and negotiable prices. There are a few souvenir shops along Abdulla Bin Thani Street, such as Arts & Crafts, which sells a good range at reasonable prices. Most shopping malls have souvenir shops; there is an excellent one at Villaggio Mall (p.135) called Qatar Souvenirs (446 6153), and there are often in-mall exhibitions that showcase the region's favourite types of souvenirs.

Tailoring & Textiles

As a stopover on major trading routes, the Middle East region has always had a thriving textile market. No matter what colour or type of fabric you are looking for, there are numerous dedicated shops around Doha. Souk Al Dira (p.132) and Souk Al Asiery (p.132) have a collection of shops inside air-conditioned buildings, selling all types of fabrics. Tayif Textiles in the Souk Al Asiery is a good place to buy your material, while Lexus Tailors on Al Sadd Street is for men only. Prices tend to be a little more expensive than in individual shops, ranging from QR 30 to QR 800 per yard.

There is no shortage of tailors in Doha and once you find a good one it should be able to make up anything you want. Word of mouth is the best way to find a tailor who is competent and reliable. The tailors in the region can copy any garment, picture or pattern. Head to Al Kahraba Street or Wadi Al Musheirib Street and you will find a good range. Prices don't vary much from one place to another, although highly skilled tailors who can produce more intricate garments, like wedding dresses, are more expensive. Once you have chosen your fabric, you can show your tailor a picture of what you want or even just take in a garment for them to copy.

Clockwise from top left: Suits, Qatari weaving textiles, textile shop

Going Out

146 Doha Delights

150 Venue Directory

154 Al Sadd & Al Rayyan Road

162 Diplomatic Area & West Bay

172 Doha Corniche

176 Khalifa Street & Al Luqta Street

178 Salwa Road & Al Aziziyah

192 Souk Area & Souk Waqif

202 Entertainment

Doha Delights

It might not have the entertainment draw of other cities in the region, but Doha's nightlife is far from a bore.

Although Doha is still a relatively small city, the number of restaurants and entertainment venues is expanding rapidly. Five years ago, a business traveller looking for a nightcap would have been limited to a few empty bars in the Ramada Plaza (p.46). Things are completely different now. The Ramada is still a nightlife hub, but hardly the only option. A slew of gorgeous new hotels have raised the culinary bar for travelling gourmands. Restaurants like Il Teatro (p.166) and Mint (p.187) are on a par with anything else in the region and are a must for discerning diners. With new hotels springing up and the multi-billion dollar Pearl Qatar development beginning to open, the choice of what to eat and where to go has never been greater. With the exception of the Sealine Beach Resort (p.47), there are few desirable restaurants or hotels outside Doha, so if you want to eat out or dance the night away you need to be in the capital. If you're in town on a Friday, be sure to book yourself into one of the big hotel brunches – they're a Doha institution and all the main hotels offer lavish spreads. The Going Out section is organised by area, and each area section begins with a mini venue finder to help you find exactly what you're in the mood for. Reviews within each area are then listed in order, starting with cafes followed by restaurants, bars and clubs.

Eating Out

There is a good range of restaurants to choose from, with anything from basic budget canteen-style places to top notch designer dining. On the whole, prices are reasonable in comparison to some other parts of the world. Compared with five years ago, the number of choices has increased dramatically, and each new hotel usually brings with it a few new options. The newly renovated Souk Waqif (p.130) has also provided space for independent restaurants such as Tajine (p.200). The busiest nights are Wednesday, Thursday and Friday, so be sure to book early. Nearly all restaurants are family-friendly, and many have special family sections. If you have a food allergy – particularly to nuts, which are used a lot – you need to be careful in Doha as menus can be very vague about listing ingredients. Also, language difficulties, ignorance about food allergies and a desire to always say 'yes' to customers means that you may be told a dish is safe to eat when it isn't.

Door Policy

Most of the bars are quite relaxed with their door policies, but some do have bouncers outside. On busier nights they may get a bit picky and require you to be a member. Occasionally, depending on your nationality or the people you are with, you may be refused entry (in which case, the best option is to just take your custom elsewhere).

Drinking

For the moment, apart from a handful of private clubs, the only places where you can get alcohol are the major hotels, which is irritating if you fancy a cheap curry and a beer. You're also not allowed to buy alcohol from a store unless you have a licence, which requires, among other things, a Qatar residence visa. That said, The Pearl development is eventually expected to have licensed independent restaurants and bars. Despite the lack of independent pubs and clubs, the city houses some worthwhile drinking holes; Sky View (p.161) at La Cigale sports gorgeous views while the Admiral's Club (p.170) at the Ritz-Carlton is great for a spot of hip shaking.

Local Cuisine

Lebanese cuisine is the most commonly exported to the west, but traditional Arabic cuisines vary from country to country. Qatari cuisine is heavily influenced by Indian and Iranian foods, and one of the country's signature dishes, machbous, is very similar to the Indian biryani. Most of the Arabic restaurants in Qatar serve a version of

The Yellow Star

The little yellow star highlights venues that merit extra praise. It could be the atmosphere, the food, the cocktails, the music or the crowd, but whatever the reason, any review that you see with the star attached is somewhere considered a bit special.

Lebanese food, and some of the highlights include Automatic (p.157) and Al Liwan (p.194). Unfortunately, restaurants serving traditional Qatari food are rare, but those keen enough to try it should check out Balhambar (p.173) or Al Majlis (p.156).

Shisha Cafes

It is common in this part of the world to see men, and some women, of all ages relaxing in the evening with a coffee or juice and a shisha pipe. For visitors and residents, even non-smokers, it's one of those must-do experiences and could just become a regular pastime. Many of the Arabic cafes and restaurants around town have shisha available and it makes a perfect end to a meal, especially when sitting outdoors – try Al Wanis Shisha Terrace (425 6243) at Sharq Village & Spa for a spot with great views. If you fancy buying your own then the souks (p.128) are a good place to start, but most souvenir shops sell shisha pipes, as do the larger supermarkets.

Vegetarian Food
Meat plays heavily in Arabic mains, but many of the Arabic appetisers, such as hummus, babba ganoosh and the various salads, are vegetarian. Also, many of the American or European chain restaurants are used to catering to non-meat eaters and will always have a vegetarian option on the menu. There are also plenty of independent Indian restaurants which serve only vegetarian food, often very cheaply.

Cafes

Café Plus	p.179
Caffe Amici	p.163
Cinnzeo	p.163
Coffea	p.155
Costa Coffee	p.164
Cup & Cino Coffee House	p.155
Eli France	p.180
JG Sandwich Cellar	p.193
La Cremiera	p.193
La Dolce Vita!	p.164
Le Pain Quotidien	p.180
Lina's	p.180
Paul	p.181
Sheraton Park Cafe	p.172
THE One	p.176

Restaurants

American	Applebee's	p.181
	Chili's	p.183
	Fuddruckers	p.177
	Johnny Rockets	p.185
	Ponderosa	p.188
	TGI Friday's	p.177
Arabic	Al Hamra	p.156
	Al Khaima	p.156
	Al Liwan	p.194
	Al Majlis	p.156

	Al Shaheen	p.165
	Albatross	p.194
	Assaha Lebanese Cultural Village	p.195
⭐	Automatic	p.157
⭐	Balhambar	p.173
	Beirut	p.173
	Kebab King	p.196
⭐	Layali Restaurant	p.186
	The Tent	p.200
Chinese	Beijing	p.182
	Chopsticks	p.157
	Ruby Wu's	p.188
Far Eastern	Asia Live!	p.195
	Thai Noodles	p.200
	Thai Snacks	p.160
	Wok Mee	p.168
French	Brasserie On The Beach	p.166
	Fauchon	p.185
⭐	La Mer	p.167
	Maxim	p.187
Indian	Asha's	p.182
	Bombay Balti	p.183
	Bukhara	p.177
⭐	Chingari	p.184
	Star of India	p.158
⭐	Taj Rasoi	p.199
	The Garden	p.196

International	Al Hubara	p.164
	Cafe Batteel	p.183
	Crepaway	p.184
	Grand Gourmet	p.157
	Layali Lounge	p.186
	Le Cigalon	p.158
	Le Monot	p.186
	Mint Living Cafe & Restaurant	p.187
	Neo	p.187
	Richoux	p.168
	The Lagoon	p.167
Italian	All'Aperto	p.195
	Ciao	p.184
	Il Rustico	p.173
	Il Teatro	p.166
	Porcini	p.168
	The Italian Job	p.185
	Za Moda	p.169
Japanese	Sakura	p.188
	Yen Sushi Bar	p.160
Mediterranean	Corniche	p.196
	La Villa	p.198
	Le Central	p.158
	Seasons	p.199
Mexican	Salsa	p.198
Moroccan	Tajine	p.200
	Tangia	p.160

Persian	Ras Al Nasaa	p.174
Seafood	Al Dana	p.194
	Al Sayyad	p.165
	Fish Market	p.166
Steakhouse	Bentley's Grill	p.182
	The Old Manor	p.198
Tex Mex	Paloma	p.167

Bars

	Aussie Legends	p.174
	Bubbles	p.190
	Cigar Lounge	p.201
	Garvey's	p.190
	Habanos	p.170
	Irish Harp	p.169
	Madison Piano Bar	p.161
	Piano Piano	p.201
	Shehrazad Lounge Bar & Terrace	p.191
	Sky View	p.161
	Spikes Lounge	p.169
	The Library	p.190
	The Library Bar & Cigar Lounge	p.170

Nightclubs

	Admiral's Club	p.170
	CloudNYN	p.161
	Qube	p.191
	The Pearl Lounge Club	p.201

Al Sadd & Al Rayyan Road

Some of the country's best Arabic restaurants are located in this area, as are the posh restaurants in Le Cigale Hotel.

Al Sadd is one of Doha's oldest communities and the bustling Al Rayyan Road is its main artery. Several of the city's best known Arabic restaurants are located here, and have been for quite some time. New to Al Sadd is the Lebanese-run Le Cigalon which, since opening in 2008, has quickly become a haven for the city's trendy media-types. For a classic Doha night, treat yourself to Yen's rotating sushi bar (p.160), then head upstairs to sip cocktails from Sky View's terrace (p.161) until the wee-hours. Top it all off with one of the Middle East's most popular shawarmas at Automatic (p.157).

Venue Finder

Cafe	Coffea	p.155
Cafe	Cup & Cino Coffee House	p.155
Arabic	Al Hamra	p.156
Arabic	Al Khaima	p.156
Arabic	Al Majlis	p.156
Arabic	⭐ Automatic	p.157
Chinese	Chopsticks	p.157
Far Eastern	Thai Snacks	p.160
Indian	Star of India	p.158

International	Grand Gourmet	p.157
International	Le Cigalon	p.158
Japanese	Yen Sushi Bar	p.160
Mediterranean	Le Central	p.158
Moroccan	Tangia	p.160
Bar	Madison Piano Bar	p.161
Bar	Sky View	p.161
Nightclub	CloudNYN	p.161

Cafes

Coffea

Royal Plaza   413 0375

Located on the third floor of Royal Plaza, this friendly spot is a tranquil option for a rest after a hard morning's credit card bashing. You can sit in the cafe or just beyond, where it is nice, light and airy. The coffee is particularly good, and there is also a range of pastries and light snacks. Map 4 C2

Cup & Cino Coffee House

Royal Plaza   413 0375

Comfortable furnishings and subdued lighting combine to make this intimate cafe a pleasant getaway where shoppers can relax. The windows are adorned with simple cherrywood blinds and the outside tables have umbrellas to provide something of a Parisian cafe experience. The full menu has plenty of choice, whether you're just stopping by for a coffee or are in need of some more substantial sustenance. Map 4 C2

Restaurants

Al Hamra
Al Rayyan Road

Arabic

443 3297

Al Hamra offers casual dining with a full Arabic menu, and makes a great place to stop by for a quick bite. It is close to the souks (behind Al Reem Pharmacy) and is popular with weary shoppers in need of a break. The fresh juices are certainly a good way to boost your energy levels. This is also a good spot for breakfast, with the thyme-flavoured breads and traditional mint tea recommended. Map 4 C1

Al Khaima
Al Sadd Road

Arabic

444 6962

Al Khaima literally translated means 'the tent', and diners here can relax in traditional tented surroundings around the clock as the restaurant is open 24 hours. Known for its quality Arabic cuisine, each dish is accompanied by fresh, oval-shaped bread. The restaurant is spacious, making it a great venue for families with children. Map 4 C2

Al Majlis
Al Sadd Road

Arabic

444 7417

The upstairs level of this popular spot has intimate cubicles with curtains, while downstairs you can dine seated on Arabic cushions and carpets. The traditional Arabic menu features mezze and grilled meats, as well as the signature hammour fish with baby shrimp and cheese. To find it, turn right after the 'White Thread' shop at the Qtel end of Al Sadd Street. Map 4 C2

Automatic

Al Sadd Road

Arabic

442 5999

The Automatic chain of restaurants has been serving great quality Arabic food in a casual setting across the Middle East for years. The menu sports a good selection of inexpensive mezzes and salads as well as grilled meat, fish and kebabs. The portions are large and are served by efficient and friendly waiting staff. Map 4 C2

Chopsticks

Grand Regency Hotel

Chinese

434 3333

In a pleasant setting befitting this smart hotel, Chopsticks is on the lobby level of the Grand Regency. The restaurant serves all the usual favourites from the orient, expertly prepared in an authentic style. The menu features a good selection of rice and noodle dishes, suitable for both vegetarians and meat-eaters. It is open for lunch and dinner, but does not serve alcohol. Map 4 C1

Grand Gourmet

Grand Regency Hotel

International

434 3333

Grand Gourmet serves up an array of contemporary global cuisine from international culinary masters. The food, the surroundings and the atmosphere are yours to savour all day long in this exquisite buffet and a la carte restaurant. Whether you want a leisurely breakfast, a power lunch or a candlelit dinner, with friendly staff and faultless fare you'll find the experience as grand as the restaurant's name. Map 4 C1

Le Central
La Cigale

Mediterranean
428 8888

Surrounded on three sides by floor-to-ceiling glass, Le Central offers great views and is so bright you may need sunglasses. You can order off the a la carte menu, or opt for the three-course business lunch which changes every week. Try the steamed hammour fish, a healthy, tasty dish served from its foil parcel at the table. You can also pay QR 90 to eat from the salad bar, which isn't piled high like some buffets. At night, with the lights of Doha twinkling around you, it's an atmospheric location. Map 4 D2

Le Cigalon
La Cigale

International
428 8888

This bright and modern buffet restaurant features a giant aquarium alongside amber and grey leather seats. The emphasis is on Lebanese food with unusual dishes like kibbeh shishbarak (couscous and meat patties cooked in yoghurt). La Cigale flies in most of its fresh food from Lebanon every day, and if you like it you can also buy it from the traiteur (food hall) next door – it isn't cheap, but it is impressive. Map 4 D2

Star of India
Near TV & Radio Roundabout

Indian
486 4440

The Star of India's tasty dishes are popular among they city's many curry connoisseurs. The restaurant has a family oriented atmosphere and there is a separate party hall for groups of 35 or more guests. The decor is simple and relaxed, and the place offers satisfying, value-for-money food. Map 2 C4

Clockwise from top left: Le Cigalon, Le Central, Sky View

Qatar Mini Visitors' Guide

Tangia
Grand Regency Hotel

Moroccan
434 3333

Tangia strives to recreate the sights, sounds, smells and tastes of exotic Morocco. The dishes dispatched by the skilled chef contain unique flavours and aromas, and all are artistically prepared and extravagantly served. The scent of coriander, cumin and saffron, mingling with the stark aroma of olive oil, adds to the experience, making Tangia the jewel of this hotel. Map 4 C1

Thai Snacks
Al Mirqab Al Jadeed Street

Far Eastern
432 9704

The interior of Thai Snacks is basic, but the food is fresh, hot and tasty. You can eat inside or outside in the pretty garden which is screened from the road. Should you also need your stiff neck sorting out, you can get a Thai massage next door. Thai Snacks is located next to Champs Elyseés gift shop at the C-Ring Road end of Al Mirqab. Map 4 C2

Yen Sushi Bar
La Cigale

Japanese
428 8888

Located in La Cigale's lobby, this intimate sushi bar can only accommodate 18 people around its rotating belt. Diners can peer over the moving sashimi and watch the masterful chefs prepare some of the best sushi in town beneath fibre-optic lighting. Ultra-contemporary bar stools round out the futuristic setting. A few tables line the perimeter of the bar, but be sure to sit up close if you want to enjoy the full experience. Map 4 D2

Bars

Madison Piano Bar

La Cigale   428 8888

A vaulted, fibre-optic laden ceiling hovers over fashionable media types lounging in red leather chairs – a combination reeking of new money and expensive tastes. Drinks aren't cheap, and tables must be reserved for weekends, but if you want to be seen, this is the place to come. Map 4 D2

Sky View

La Cigale   428 8888

This is the trendiest bar in Doha. Head through a nondescript door on the fifteenth floor and suddenly you're on a huge balcony enjoying the coolest view in town. There is a DJ and a real buzz about the place – this is where the beautiful people hang out. Snacks like sushi and sashimi are also served, but you have to book or you have no chance of getting in. Map 4 D2

Nightclubs

CloudNYN

Merweb Hotel   436 9555

One of the more affordable clubs in Doha, CloudNYN tends to appeal to a young and diverse crowd. Couples and women get in free, but single men pay QR 50. The club runs plenty of offers – usually involving free drinks for women. Smart jeans are ok and you'll need an ID to get in. The club is open every night from 18:00 until 03:00. Map 4 C2

Diplomatic Area & West Bay

With the country's best mall and several of the most popular hotels, the Diplomatic area has become a hub for fine dining and friendly cafes.

It's hard to imagine that just a few years ago the City Center Mall was the only recognisable landmark north of the Corniche. Today, the shore of the Diplomatic Area is lined with five-star hotels that feature gorgeously decorated restaurants serving equally impressive food. Head further north to the West Bay and you'll experience much of the same. With names like the Four Seasons and the Ritz-Carlton, it's no wonder that this is the fine dining capital of the city.

Venue Finder

Cafe	Caffe Amici	p.163
Cafe	Cinnzeo	p.163
Cafe	Costa Coffee	p.164
Cafe	La Dolce Vita!	p.164
Arabic	Al Shaheen	p.165
Far Eastern	Wok Mee	p.168
French	Brasserie On The Beach	p.166
French	La Mer	p.167
International	Al Hubara	p.164
International	The Lagoon	p.167
International	Richoux	p.168
Italian	Il Teatro	p.166
Italian	Porcini	p.168

Italian	Za Moda	p.169
Seafood	Al Sayyad	p.165
Seafood	⭐ Fish Market	p.166
Tex Mex	Paloma	p.167
Bar	⭐ Irish Harp	p.169
Bar	Spikes Lounge	p.169
Cigar Bar	⭐ Habanos	p.170
Cigar Bar	The Library Bar & Cigar Lounge	p.170
Nightclub	Admiral's Club	p.170

Cafes

Caffe Amici

City Center Doha   483 4811

In the midst of the jewellery shops at the far end of City Center, Caffe Amici is a haven of calm. The biggest draw has to be the comfy armchairs where you can take the weight off your feet and forget about shopping for a while. The staff are great and there is a good selection of croissants, sandwiches and cakes, making it perfect for afternoon tea. Map 3 D2

Cinnzeo

City Center Doha   483 9990

This international cake and coffee shop chain has the stickiest cinnamon buns around. Enjoy a tasty bun with a freshly brewed cup of American coffee as a treat when you're all shopped out, but there are only four seats so it's just the lucky ones that get to sit down and relax. The branches in The Mall and Hyatt Plaza are more generous with tables and chairs. Map 3 D2

Costa Coffee

City Center Doha 469 7961

International chain Costa offers a wide selection of coffee brewed to a traditional Italian recipe. There is a good tea menu, and it serves up huge hot chocolates if you feel like a treat. The long list of cold, coffee based drinks is popular, and flavours often change with the seasons. Costa also has a good pastry selection, including mini tasters. Other locations include Jarir Bookstore (436 6724) and The Centre (441 7869). Map 3 D2

La Dolce Vita!

The Ritz-Carlton Doha 484 8000

La Dolce Vita! coffee shop is an ideal place to meet your friends or business acquaintances for a chat, and to treat yourself to something from the wide selection of coffees, teas and mouthwatering home-made cakes. The shelves are packed with gourmet foods such as caviar, foie gras, oils and teas from around the world, any of which make the perfect present for gastronomic connoisseurs. Map 2 E1

Restaurants

Al Hubara

Sheraton Doha Hotel & Resort International
485 4444

Al Hubara restaurant is open for breakfast, lunch and dinner. Served buffet style, there is a good range of international cuisine to choose from, including Arabic, Japanese and Italian dishes. The restaurant has a separate room for families, which doubles as a non-smoking area. This is a popular venue for lunchtime meetings, as well as for those seeking a lingering break from work. Map 3 E3

Al Sayyad
Dimplomatic Club

Seafood
484 7444

For a relaxing night out of town this restaurant is a good choice. Set just off the beach at the Diplomatic Club, with outside seating for the cooler months, it offers a great choice of seafood. Sit back and enjoy the authentic Arabic salads while you take your pick from the menu. If you can't decide, the waiters are on hand with helpful advice. Map 2 E1

Al Shaheen
Sheraton Doha

Arabic
485 4444

Set on the top floor of the pyramid-shaped Sheraton Hotel, this restaurant enjoys impressive views of the city and coastline. The traditional live entertainment can be a little overbearing, but don't let this put you off as the food is beautifully presented and portions are ample. For less adventurous diners there are western dishes as well. Map 3 E3

Afternoon Tea

It's hard to imagine a more luxurious activity than taking afternoon tea. Several of the top hotels in the city offer high tea and some of the standouts include Al Jalsa at Sharq Village Hotel & Spa (425 6666), The Lobby Lounge at the Ritz-Carlton (484 8000) and Seasons Tea Lounge at the Four Seasons (494 8888). Each venue handles the tradition flawlessly and elegantly – a Doha must.

Brasserie On The Beach

French

Four Seasons Hotel

494 8888

Although the Brasserie is not actually on the beach, it does overlook the hotel's attractive gardens. Open throughout the day, this buffet style restaurant serves the usual array of soups and salads, and a variety of meat and fish dishes. It is slightly more expensive than its neighbours, but the service cannot be faulted. It's certainly a suitable venue for a business lunch or dinner with clients. Map 3 F2

Fish Market

Seafood

InterContinental Doha

484 4444

Instead of reading the menu, pick your fresh fish and vegetables from market-style displays and have the chef cook it however you like. Some people love this, but others prefer not to eyeball their fish on the ice before eating it. The restaurant is in a great setting on the edge of the beach. For a romantic evening in the cooler months, sit on the covered terrace and enjoy the sea views and starry sky. Map 2 E2

Il Teatro

Italian

Four Seasons Hotel

494 8888

The glass-encased wine cellar and harpist are clear signs that Il Teatro strives to impress. Glass sculptures splash the room with colour, while marble floors and wood trim create a subdued atmosphere. The food is modern Italian, and might just be the best in Doha. Even on the busiest nights, the attentive waiting staff seem to anticipate your every move. The all-Italian wine list is impressive, offering plenty of variety. Map 3 F2

La Mer
French

The Ritz-Carlton Doha
484 8503

On the top floor of the Ritz-Carlton, La Mer has exceptional views of Doha's waterfront and The Pearl Qatar development. This is a classy joint, with gleaming silverware, fine china, sparkling chandeliers and faultless French cuisine – it's surely a contender for the ultimate dining experience in Qatar. The restaurant's layout is perfect for both a pre-dinner drink or a full-blown dining experience. Map 2 E1

The Lagoon
International

The Ritz-Carlton Doha
484 8000

Open all day and bursting at the seams with choices, the temptation here is to try it all. With live cooking stations, the talented chefs will prepare certain dishes freshly to order. As you would expect from the Ritz-Carlton, the food is beautifully presented and the service is impeccable. The Friday brunch is particularly popular, especially with families. Map 2 E1

Paloma
Tex Mex

InterContinental Doha
484 4444

A spicy Latino atmosphere awaits everyone at this lively Mexican restaurant where good food, entertainment and a superb choice of drinks are found in abundance. The interior is dominated by the large bar and dancefloor – it feels like a bar with food rather than a restaurant with drinks, so is a bit different for Doha. If the generally good band is a bit much for your tastes, a quieter evening can be enjoyed on the outside terrace overlooking the pool. Map 3 F2

Porcini

Italian

The Ritz-Carlton Doha

484 8000

Porcini's welcoming ambience creates the perfect venue for a romantic dinner or entertaining clients. The decor is rich and warm, and the open kitchen is framed by a mosaic of coloured glass tiles. With the emphasis on classical Italian cuisine, the menu features fresh bread, home-made pasta, salads, seafood and meat dishes, as well as tempting desserts. Wine lovers will be pleased with the broad range of vintages. Map 2 E1

Richoux

International

City Center Doha

493 1661

Richoux's dark woodwork, red leather seats and gold-coloured railings and light fittings are a world away from the shops just outside. One side of the menu features breakfast, drinks, pastries, and a full traditional afternoon tea for two. Flip the menu over and you'll find a choice of sandwiches, starters and mains. There's terrace seating at the front, but it may be a little noisy for some. Map 3 D2

Wok Mee

Far Eastern

Mövenpick Tower & Suites

496 6600

This newish restaurant has a great atmosphere, a modern unfussy interior and lovely lighting. The chefs work behind a glass wall, with the daily specials chalked up beside them. The ingredients are zingy fresh and the meat is possibly the best in Doha. The lovely staff will patiently talk you through the long menu. This hotel is dry, but the mocktails are pretty good and the ginger and lemongrass water is delicious. Map 3 F2

Za Moda
Italian

InterContinental Doha
484 4444

Za Moda's interior is fresh and clean, modern without trying too hard. The menu features mostly traditional dishes with a few creative touches. The short list of ingredients in the ravioli with sage and butter lets you taste how fresh the food really is. Follow that with the sorbet and berries and you're sure to make a return trip. Map 3 E2

Bars

Irish Harp
Sheraton Hotel
454 4444

Descend to the basement of the Sheraton and you enter another world. The Irish Harp is one of the multitude of fake Irish pubs that have popped up around the globe. It looks the part – an old-fashioned bar with frosted windows, Guinness on tap and decent bar meals. It's busy with a good atmosphere and friendly staff. Only the Filipino band and the fact you're allowed to smoke tell you you're not in Ireland. Map 3 E3

Spikes Lounge
Doha Golf Club
496 0777

Spikes Lounge, on the ground floor of the club house, has a relaxed and easy atmosphere, with drinks and good food. The outside seating overlooks the course and is great during the winter months. Thankfully, the inside is just as pleasant, with comfy sofas to rest your weary bones on while you wait for your drinks to arrive. Map 2 D1

Habanos
The Ritz-Carlton Doha

Cigar Bar
484 8503

With rich reds and dark mahogany, Habanos has an intimate and cosy feel, and in the cooler weather you can relax outside on the attractive terrace. The cocktails are divine, and little touches like the complimentary snacks add to the experience. The bar has its own 'cigar butler' who will make recommendations and cut and light cigars for you. Map 2 E1

The Library Bar & Cigar Lounge
Four Seasons Hotel

Cigar Bar
494 8888

Surrounded by leather buttoned chairs and comfy sofas, you can't help but relax at the Library Bar. Abstract art hanging from the dark wood walls adds to the ambience of the gentlemen's club setting. Take your pick from the cigar and food menu while enjoying the splendid sea views, or the music from the pianist who plays every night from 20:00. Map 3 F2

Nightclubs

Admiral's Club
The Ritz-Carlton Doha

484 8000

Set away from the hotel in a separate building by the marina, this popular club seems to pick up around 23:00 and goes on till 03:00. During the cooler months, it has a wonderful outdoor space overlooking the yachts moored below. Open on Thursday and Friday nights only, non-members must pay a QR 150 entrance fee, which includes a drink. The dress code is described as 'elegant', but smart jeans are ok. Map 2 E1

Doha Corniche

With spectacular views of the rising Doha skyline, the few restaurants along the Corniche hold a distinct advantage.

It's surprising that more restaurants and cafes have not opened up along the Corniche, but the lack of clutter is what makes the area so appealing. The few restaurants located on the grass-lined avenue are well worth a visit as they provide an opportunity to soak up the ascending skyline and calm waters.

Venue Finder

Cafe	Sheraton Park Cafe	p.172
Arabic	⭐ Balhambar	p.173
Arabic	Beirut	p.173
Italian	Il Rustico	p.173
Persian	Ras Al Nasaa	p.174
Sports Bar	Aussie Legends	p.174

Cafes

Sheraton Park Cafe

Sheraton Park

The menu at this tiny cafe on the northern-most tip of the Corniche is limited, but its setting in the picturesque Sheraton Park makes it a worthwhile end to any Corniche trip. The tea is good enough, but stay away from the coffee. By far the best thing on the menu is the fresh juice selection. Map 3 E3

Restaurants

Balhambar
The Corniche

Arabic
483 4423

Set on the Corniche with waterfront views, Balhambar is well known for offering traditional Qatari cooking in an equally traditional setting. The waiters, all in national dress, are attentive and friendly, and the building's wind towers outside and gypsum walls inside are typical of the region. The restaurant is known for two Qatari dishes: ghuzi, a whole roasted lamb served on a bed of rice with pine nuts, and harees, a slow-cooked wheat and lamb dish. Map 3 C4

Beirut
Al Kahraba St

Arabic
442 1087

Feel like a local by pulling your car up to the front door of this predominantly takeaway restaurant. Soon enough, a waiter will run out to your car window to take your order. Serving a good selection of Lebanese food, Beirut is known to many residents for its fabulous hummus and foul, a traditional bean dish popular throughout the Arab world. Map 5 B3

Il Rustico
Rydges Plaza

Italian
438 5444

This low-key restaurant is not necessarily intimate, secluded or romantic, but it is a popular venue offering great Mediterranean fare in pleasant surroundings. The menu is good for meat, pasta and pizza lovers, but vegetarians may be a little disappointed. Meals start with a DIY garlic bread platter, tasty but not recommended if you have an early morning meeting the next day. The wine list is substantial, as are the desserts. Map 5 A1

Ras Al Nasaa

Persian

The Corniche   441 1177

Nestling beneath and beyond the traditional windtowers near Museum Roundabout, this is not one restaurant, but a complex of eateries that has something for most tastes. The small coffee shop is pleasant enough, and there is a big family hall with impressive terracotta arches. The bachelors' hall is reserved just for the boys (think TV, shisha and comfy sofas), and the floating pontoon restaurant offers good views across the water. The real star is the Qasr Al Sahel Iranian restaurant, serving traditional Persian dishes in a cosy setting. Map 5 F2

Bars

Aussie Legends

Sports Bar

Rydges Plaza   438 5444

The mood and atmosphere here varies depending on the night of the week. At weekends the place is busy, a popular spot for expats to socialise, enjoy a few drinks, and dance if there's a live band playing. If you come during the week, however, you may find yourself surrounded by lone hotel guests sipping a pint while watching sports on one of the many big screens. There isn't much in terms of ambience, but the drinks are reasonably priced and the bar snacks are tasty. Map 5 A1

Ras Al Nasaa

Khalifa Street & Al Luqta Street

What Khalifa Street lacks in gourmet dining it makes up for with a host of cheap cafeterias, serving some of the best juices in town.

The Khalifa-Al Luqta corridor may be short on big name eateries, but if you seek a cheap curry or the experience of walking into a budget cafeteria, this area is one of your best bets. Despite their shabbiness, the small cafeterias are usually clean. They also serve amazing fresh juices for practically nothing.

Venue Finder

Cafe	THE One	p.176
Indian	Bukhara	p.177
American	Fuddruckers	p.177
American	TGI Friday's	p.177

Cafes

THE One

Landmark Shopping Mall   488 8669

This cafe is a hip getaway situated within THE One furniture store. Stylishly decorated, as you would expect from Doha's trendiest furniture shop, it is popular all day long. The menu is quirky and makes for a refreshing change from the usual cafe fare. An added attraction is that if you like the furniture, silverware or china, you can buy them in the store. Map 2 B3

Restaurants

Bukhara
Near Khalifa Tennis Complex

Indian

483 3345

Bukhara's soft lighting and friendly staff aptly give way to the restaurant's main feature – the tandoor oven, which is visible for all to see as the chef works his magic in the open-air kitchen. The food is lovely, and the freshly baked naan breads are mouthwateringly good. If you enjoy great-tasting, good value Indian food, then this is a must-visit place. Map 3 B4

Fuddruckers
Near Khalifa Tennis Complex

American

483 3983

Children are provided with an elaborate play space outside, allowing the grown ups some relative peace and quiet in the Americana themed dining area. Portions are massive and Fuddruckers particularly prides itself on its steaks and burgers. Wash it all down with bottomless sodas and shakes. Map 3 B4

TGI Friday's
Landmark Shopping Mall

American

486 6602

This popular American theme restaurant offers a fun dining experience, flowing drinks and a lively atmosphere. The square bar area is always busy, and a perfect spot to meet for a (non-alcoholic) drink before making for your table. If you're the first to arrive, the uniformed bar staff will keep you entertained, twirling bottles as they serve. There is another TGIF in Villaggio Mall (450 7288). Map 2 B3

Salwa Road & Al Aziziyah

With the massive Ramada Plaza complex at its start, this is the default hub of Doha nightlife. Bars, restaurants and independent cafes abound.

The Ramada Plaza Doha has long been the centre of Doha dining. With 20 bars and restaurants, the plaza has something for everyone. If you've had your fill of hotel dining, there are several independent restaurants and cafes in the immediate area and along Salwa Road, including the design-conscious Mint (p.187) and surprisingly authentic Layali (p.186).

Venue Finder

Cafe	Café Plus	p.179
Cafe	Eli France	p.180
Cafe	Le Pain Quotidien	p.180
Cafe	Lina's	p.180
Cafe	Paul	p.181
American	Applebee's	p.181
American	Chili's	p.183
American	Johnny Rockets	p.185
American	Ponderosa	p.188
Arabic	★ Layali Restaurant	p.186
Chinese	Beijing	p.182
Chinese	Ruby Wu's	p.188
French	Fauchon	p.185
French	Maxim	p.187

Indian	Asha's	p.182
Indian	Bombay Balti	p.183
Indian	⭐ Chingari	p.184
International	Cafe Batteel	p.183
International	⭐ Crepaway	p.184
International	Layali Lounge	p.186
International	Le Monot	p.186
International	⭐ Mint Living Cafe & Restaurant	p.187
International	Neo	p.187
Italian	Ciao	p.184
Italian	The Italian Job	p.185
Japanese	⭐ Sakura	p.188
Steakhouse	Bentley's Grill	p.182
Bar	Bubbles	p.190
Bar	The Library	p.190
Bar	Shehrazad Lounge Bar & Terrace	p.191
Bar	Garvey's	p.190
Nightclub	Qube	p.191

Cafes

Café Plus

The Centre   441 6539

It's easy to miss this pleasant cafe, which is tucked away
behind the Scholl shop. Very large and airy, it boasts vast
glass windows and plenty of space between tables. Plus
makes all its own cakes, including the divine carrot variety.
The sandwiches are huge and the crepes are wafer thin and
golden brown. The icecream is home-made too. Map 4 D2

Eli France

Salwa Road   435 7222

Eli France is known for its bakery, but also offers a surprisingly full international menu. It serves breakfast, sandwiches, snacks, burgers, a selection of main dishes, home-made desserts and freshly squeezed juices. There's also a kids' menu and another branch in City Center Doha. Map 4 A3

Le Pain Quotidien

Villaggio Mall   413 5245

This Belgian cafe manages to pull off the trick of pretending not to be in a shopping mall. The inside seating is the best option, as outside in the mall can be noisy. The bread and coffee are organic and good quality. Breakfast consists of lovely croissants and bread, fresh butter and nice jams. The open sandwiches have some unusual combinations which work very well, like egg salad with anchovies and halloumi with pesto. Map 4 D2

Lina's

Near Micmac Flyover   436 5488

Known for its sandwiches and home-made breads, Lina's has a simple, relaxed feel and attentive staff. Keep abreast of world news via the plasma-screen TVs, or catch up on your emails by hooking up to the Wi-Fi connection. The comfortable seating and well-lit interior make it an appealing office away from the office. It is situated just beyond Cafe Bateel heading towards Decoration Roundabout. Map 4 C3

Paul

Villaggio Mall 413 5508

Despite being in the middle of a shopping centre in Doha, this cafe, with its mismatched chairs and tables, and glass awning, does manage to feel quite French. A good place for a weekend breakfast, Paul also does a nice range of salads, sandwiches and main courses. There is a children's menu, but sometimes the choice is limited. Map 4 A3

Restaurants

Applebee's American

Nr Ramada Junction 436 0747

Geared towards families, the large menu should please all tastes. The restaurant has a young, vibrant feel to it, with energetic staff. The shared appetiser dishes are always fun, but beware, the portions are huge. Map 4 D2

Power Brunch

Friday brunch is offered at most of the main hotels in Doha, making for a great family day out. Hotels usually make a special effort on Fridays and their buffet displays can be spectacular. Some restaurants will even provide entertainment for the children, giving parents a chance to relax and enjoy an extravagant spread featuring a variety of international cuisines. You usually pay a set price for all you can eat, and occasionally free drinks are included, so for those with a large appetite they definitely provide value for money.

Asha's
Villagio Mall

Indian
451 7867

It is worth opting for a table inside at this restaurant, away from the noise of the foodcourt, so you can enjoy the atmosphere. The staff are well informed about the unique dishes and are keen to recommend their favourites. The rogan josh is subtle but spicy and there are some unusual breads too, like the butter-laden lacha paratha. End with the dessert selection, where you get four substantial Indian puddings. Map 4 A3

Beijing
Opposite The Centre

Chinese
435 8688

This independent restaurant is nestled in a private villa off the busy Salwa Road. It has both indoor and outdoor seating which is suitable for large groups, as well as more intimate private dining areas separated by cubicles. Beijing has friendly, knowledgeable staff who can help you choose from the extensive menu, which features a good selection of great tasting traditional Chinese favourites. Map 4 D2

Bentley's Grill
Ramada Plaza Doha

Steakhouse
428 1428

This steakhouse's high-back leather chairs, low lighting and dark wood trim resemble a setting in a gangster film. The small dining area can be stuffy at peak times, but the overall feel is intimate. Not surprisingly, the menu revolves around meat and traditional steakhouse sides like steamed vegetables and potatoes. The waiting staff are responsive, but not as quick as you'd expect in this sort of venue. Map 4 D2

Bombay Balti

Indian
Ramada Plaza Doha — 428 1428

This informal but stylish restaurant is downstairs in the new wing of the Ramada Plaza and offers British Indian restaurant-style curries, including old favourites like balti, dopiaza and rogan josh. The menu is brief, but that saves time on dithering – the food is good and the service is friendly. Bombay Balti is popular so book in advance, especially at the weekend. Map 4 D2

Cafe Batteel

International
Salwa Road — 444 1414

As you head out of Doha on Salwa Road, Cafe Batteel is easy to miss, but worth seeking out. Menu options include superb salads, soups and sandwiches, plus heartier main courses that take cues from India, Italy and Arabia. The interior features wooden alcoves, Arabic cushions and barasti palm ceilings. Upstairs is the family room, as well as a computer-games room where the kids will keep themselves entertained for hours. Map 4 D3

Chili's

American
Nr Ramada Junction — 444 5335

Known for its massive portions and signature burgers, this popular American chain has made its mark on Qatar. The atmosphere is relaxed with western background music to enjoy. You'd be forgiven for forgetting you're still in the Middle East while you enjoy your massive country fried steak. You can also find Chili's in The Mall (p.137). Map 4 D2

Going Out

Salwa Road & Al Aziziyah

Chingari
Ramada Plaza Doha

Indian
428 1428

Chingari is one of the most popular Indian restaurants in Doha. It is known for its plush red room with cosy cushions that allow you to sit in comfort close to the ground. The rich curries that appear from the kitchen are absolutely cracking, and the atmosphere is wonderfully exotic, with a traditional Indian band playing background music. If you are in a large group you can ask for a private room. Map 4 D2

Ciao
Haya Complex

Italian
468 9100

This centrally located independent restaurant goes the extra mile to provide a true taste of Italia, right down to having its cheeses specially flown in. The pizzas and calzones are cooked in an open oven on the main level of the restaurant. When it comes to desserts, the tiramisu cannot be missed, although it faces stiff competition from the gelato. Map 4 A3

Crepaway
Al Mouthanna Complex

International
465 5830

As the name suggests, the menu here features a large, lip-smacking selection of sweet and savoury crepes. Open for breakfast, lunch and dinner, it also serves salads, sandwiches, pizzas, pastas and desserts. The good food is matched by the good mood, and the jukebox and live DJ produce the feel of a fun, young and upbeat diner. Map 4 D3

Fauchon
Souk Najd

French
432 4888

Although it markets itself as a true tea house, Fauchon specialises in various areas. As well as serving gourmet teas, coffees and pastries, it dishes up some of the most decadent desserts in the city, and its cakes make impressive gifts. This cafe also does very good outside catering. Map 4 D3

The Italian Job
Ramada Plaza Doha

Italian
441 1428

This is a wonderful two-floor restaurant that has a distinct rustic feel to it. The open-air kitchen allows all the beautiful aromas to spill into the main dining areas. The menu features the usual Italian treats, and the pizzas (especially the calzones) are particularly recommended. The unusual brand of musical entertainment, where the servers sing to the guests, make this an interactive dinner venue for all to enjoy. Map 4 D2

Johnny Rockets
Salwa Road

American
455 2792

Johnny Rockets attempts to recreate the atmosphere of a classic American diner, complete with colourful 1950s-style booths and enthusiastic singing staff (put *YMCA* on the jukebox and see what happens). The menu is loaded with traditional favourites including burgers, hot dogs, chicken dishes and thick milkshakes. Between 07:00 and 13:00 the restaurant offers a full breakfast menu featuring such delights as French toast and pancakes. Map 4 D2

Salwa Road & Al Aziziyah

Layali Lounge
International

Villagio Mall
451 7587

Located at the end of the canal in this smart shopping centre, this is the sister to the Lebanese Layali restaurant (below) and sports an international menu with sandwiches, pizza, salads and sushi, as well as Lebanese mezze. It has great quirky chandeliers and is smart and modern, but still quite comfortable. An unlikely hit is the brilliant English apple crumble. Sit facing the windows for some good people watching. Map 4 D3

Layali Restaurant
Arabic

Opposite Nissan dealer
431 0005

If you are looking for a truly authentic Lebanese experience, then Layali is a must. The food is impeccable and the staff, in their smart black uniforms, are polished and extremely attentive. Many people go for the wide selection of Arabic mezzes, either hot or cold, but the grilled meats and fish are the real stars. Layali is also known to have some of the best shisha in town. Map 4 A3

Le Monot
International

Ramada Junction
467 7748

Despite being situated in the busy dining hub that is the Ramada Junction, Le Monot has managed to establish itself as something of a getaway. After climbing the stairs, you'll be met by soft lighting, a cosy interior, relaxing background music and friendly staff. With a good selection of fresh and tasty dishes, this popular Italian/French-style bistro is best known for its elaborate and well-stocked salad bar. Map 4 D2

Maxim
French

Ramada Plaza Doha
428 155

The plush decor of this French restaurant features dark panelled walls, red carpets, white linen table cloths, silver cutlery and chandeliers. The menu offers a good choice of traditional continental dishes, and sorbet is served between courses to refresh the palate. The main courses are wheeled to your table and served from a trolley, and the service is prompt and not too intrusive. Map 4 D2

Mint Living Cafe & Restaurant
International

Al Muthanna Complex, Salwa Road
467 5577

Visually stunning and ever-so-hip, Mint was designed with a real eye for art and the aesthetic. The fusion menu features fresh salads, pasta, risotto, imaginative sandwiches, and generous main courses of meat and fish. The breakfast menu is also tempting, offering both continental and full English. The signature drink, lemon mint, is a surprisingly refreshing discovery, and you may just find yourself hooked. Map 4 D3

Neo
International

Opposite Nissan dealer
432 2508

Although it serves an international mix, Neo is best known for its sushi, and Tuesday is the special sushi evening. You pay a set fee and it just keeps coming; fresh, tender and undoubtedly the best in Doha. With dark wood, channels of pebbles and subdued lighting, the restaurant has a Japanese feel. Neo prides itself on preparing everything from scratch, from bread to icecream, and you'll taste the difference. Map 4 D3

Ponderosa

American

Near Ramada Junction

465 5880

Ponderosa's menu concentrates on steak, chicken and seafood dishes. The all-you-can-eat buffet is also popular throughout the day, offering American-style fare from the salad bar and self-serve icecream. There is another branch in West Bay. Map 4 D2

Ruby Wu's

Chinese

Ramada Plaza Doha

428 1428

Ruby Wu's is a popular partner restaurant to Bombay Balti (p.183), which is right next door in the same cavernous area, downstairs in the hotel's new wing. With an informal atmosphere and consistently good food, it has quickly become a regular Doha favourite. There is a good range of dishes including rice, noodles and dumplings. Map 4 D2

Sakura

Japanese

Ramada Plaza Doha

428 1428

Sitting on stools around the central teppanyaki station is the best way to appreciate the skill of the chefs who put on a real show, juggling knives, eggs, spatulas and anything else they can lay their hands on. The food is excellent, cooked to perfection and very tasty. If you fancy something a bit quieter there are a couple of small tables away from the cooking area, as well as two private rooms. Map 4 D2

Mint Living Cafe & Restaurant

Salwa Road & Al Aziziyah

Bars

Bubbles

Ramada Plaza Doha   441 7417

This champagne and cocktail bar has almost got it right. The glass wall, wacky oversized armchairs and long curving bar are smart, but there is also the usual collection of sofas which look like a job lot from Homes R Us. The cocktails are well-priced at around QR 35 and you can buy bottles of champagne for anywhere from QR 2,300 to QR 130. The bar is very busy at weekends when it's standing room only. Map 4 D2

The Library

Ramada Plaza Doha   441 7417

This quiet hideaway, on the top floor of the original wing of the Ramada, right in the heart of the city, is a great spot to get your bearings and a view. The wall panels are adorned with Egyptian hieroglyphs and, in a nod to the bar's title, the quirky bar stools and tables have legs made from stacks of books. Occasionally there is a harpist playing relaxing background music, helping all to unwind and enjoy the drinks even more. Map 4 D2

Garvey's

Off Salwa Road   450 5176

Despite being a private club, punters can usually pay a small entrance fee at the door. Always busy when there is a major sporting event on the big screens, it's the nearest thing to a local pub you'll get in Qatar. Inside is simple with plenty of room for standing around chatting. It tends to get smoky on busy nights, but you can also sit by the pool to avoid the stench. It's popular with offshore workers, or indeed anyone who fancies a good night out without five-star frills. Map 4 B4

Shehrazad Lounge Bar & Terrace
Ramada Plaza Doha　　　　　　　　441 7417
This might be one of the liveliest spots in Doha, although perhaps not one of the most cultured. There is a live band and once a month the venue hosts a popular comedy night, but whatever the occasion, this bar seems to be packed every night. For a night out with your mates and a beer or two this is a good choice – wear your jeans, have a dance, and enjoy not spending a fortune. Map 4 D2

Nightclubs

Qube
Ramada Plaza Doha　　　　441 7417
This cavernous nightclub buried deep in the Ramada complex is the newest and largest club in Doha. It offers a mixture of live music, visiting DJs and has special nights for hip-hop, UK dance and Indian music. It's got a VIP area and Doha's longest bar. The entry fee of QR 80 might be a bit steep, but it includes your first drink. Ladies get in free, and there's a ban on shorts, sandals (for men) and under 21s. Map 4 D2

Zero Tolerance

Qatar has a zero tolerance rule when it comes to driving under the influence of alcohol. Anyone caught faces huge fines and even jail time.

Souk Area & Souk Waqif

Traditional architecture and a bustling street scene make for excellent al fresco dining, while several of the city's top hotels offer indulgent fine dining.

Windtowers, stone walls and hand-sewn cushions provide an authentic backdrop for the restaurants in and around Souk Waqif. If the weather's right, choose to sit outdoors and watch the world go by the way it did a hundred years ago. Head towards the airport and you'll find the gorgeous Sharq Village & Spa (p.47), which houses some of the city's finest eateries.

Venue Finder

Cafe	JG Sandwich Cellar	p.193
Cafe	La Cremiera	p.193
Arabic	Al Liwan	p.194
Arabic	Albatross	p.194
Arabic	Assaha Lebanese Cultural Village	p.195
Arabic	Kebab King	p.196
Arabic	The Tent	p.200
Far Eastern	Asia Live!	p.195
Far Eastern	Thai Noodles	p.200
Indian	The Garden	p.196
Indian	Taj Rasoi	p.199
Italian	All'Aperto	p.195
Mediterranean	Corniche	p.196
Mediterranean	La Villa	p.198

Mediterranean	Seasons	p.199
Mexican	Salsa	p.198
Moroccan	Tajine	p.200
Seafood	⭐ Al Dana	p.194
Steakhouse	⭐ The Old Manor	p.198
Bar	Piano Piano	p.201
Bar	⭐ Cigar Lounge	p.201
Nightclub	The Pearl Lounge Club	p.201

Cafes

JG Sandwich Cellar

Near Ras Abu Roundabout   435 7559

This is a popular English-owned cafe that serves traditional
English food – and for some Brits it may feel like they have
walked straight into their mother's kitchen. JG Sandwich
Cellar is a good place to choose for a dose of comfort food
and to catch up on newspapers from home. Good sandwiches
are available and you can buy food to take away.

La Cremiera

Souk Waqif   564 3800

Head straight for the icecream at La Cremiera – it's freshly
made in the cafe every day to an Italian recipe. Take your
pick from sweet pineapple to velvety chocolate and crunchy
hazelnut. Weird and wonderful sundaes are available too,
including 'spaghetti' (squiggles of icecream) and 'pizza' (a
pancake covered in icecream, cream and fruit). You'll find La
Cremiera at the end of the main drag in Souk Waqif. Map 5 C2

Restaurants

Al Dana
Sharq Village & Spa

Seafood
425 6666

The airy, open spaces in Al Dana revolve around a beautifully laid-out fish counter in the centre. Most of the fish on display are fresh from the Gulf. The restaurant is covered in flashes of blue and turquoise. Diners can choose a fish and preparation method, order from the sushi menu, or pick and choose from the extensive a la carte selection. The best bet is to stick to the sushi and fresh fish options for your main course. Map 4 F2

Al Liwan
Sharq Village & Spa

Arabic
425 6666

Not just your average buffet, Al Liwan offers an extensive array of tasty Qatari and Arabic cuisine. Start with hot and cold Lebanese mezze, salads and bread straight from the oven. The fresh seafood and koftas are particularly good and regional main courses change regularly. The samak chermoula – kingfish with pomegranate couscous – is delicious. Those with a sweet tooth will love the well-stocked dessert station. Map 4 F2

Albatross
Al Bustan Hotel

Arabic
432 8887

This pleasant eastern-styled restaurant is popular with local families and visitors alike. The food is international with a Lebanese flavour, and the generous portions are beautifully cooked and served in a relaxed atmosphere by friendly and knowledgeable staff. Map 5 F2

All'Aperto
Marriott Doha

Italian
429 8888

All'Aperto means 'open' in Italian, and the name fits. An unpretentious but well-presented menu of pasta, pizza, and salad awaits diners at this popular open-air restaurant. Outdoor tables surrounded by clambering vines make this a great spot for a family dinner or a relaxed get-together with friends. Start with an antipasti platter while you decide on a delicious main. Map 4 F2

Asia Live!
Marriott Doha

Far Eastern
429 8888

Asia Live's popularity is partly due to the two teppanyaki cooking stations that let diners get up close to the furious slapping, chopping, throwing and catching of their soon-to-be meals. There is also a sushi bar on hand, as well as an a la carte menu. Fortunately for the romantic, the dark-wood decor and interesting layout allows for semi-private dinners. Map 4 F2

Assaha Lebanese Cultural Village
Hamad Al Kibir Street, nr Olympic Sports

Arabic
435 5353

Set in a lovely stone building, this Lebanese restaurant is designed to feel like an old village. Despite its large size, the interior feels cosy thanks to the private rooms and nooks and crannies. The grilled meats and traditional mezze are delicious, and the bread is even better. To get to it, go up Grand Hamad Street from the Corniche, cross the A Ring Road, and it's 200m on the right past Olympic Sports. Map 5 D3

Corniche
Marriott Doha

Mediterranean
429 8888

Mediterranean in style and cooking, this all-you-can-eat buffet offers a varied selection of freshly prepared dishes, but its speciality would have to be the seafood bonanza available every evening from 19:00. The setting is nice too – it's a light and airy conservatory with views of the pool and gardens. The Friday brunch is popular, with food from all over the world and entertainment for children. Map 4 F2

The Garden
Al Kahraba Street

Indian
436 5686

With cheap but well-made curry, The Garden is cleverly split into separate dining areas: downstairs for vegetarian dishes, and upstairs for a la carte or buffet style dining. The typical rich reds and golds are abundant, and there is a choice of open tables and private booths. The waiters are welcoming and full of smiles, the menu is varied, and the food is excellent. Map 5 B3

Kebab King
Near Doha International Airport

Arabic
441 0400

This is a typical kebab house with brightly coloured chairs surrounding Formica tables. The staff are friendly and helpful and the menu caters to carnivores and vegetarians alike; even the health conscious will be happy with the wide range of dishes on offer. Grilled fish and meat of various kinds are served with rice, salad or vegetables. The menu offers some very good curries as well. Map 5 D4

Top: Corniche, Bottom: Tajine

La Villa

Mediterranean

Mercure Grand Hotel Doha

446 2222

This spacious restaurant is on the 12th floor of the Mercure Grand in the heart of the city. The choice of dishes is good and some are prepared with an unexpected twist. All are creatively presented and delicious. The service is friendly, and there are great views of the bustling city below and the Doha skyline. The hotel is on Al Muntazah Street, close to the junction with Wadi Musheirib Street. Map 5 C2

The Old Manor

Steakhouse

Mercure Grand Hotel Doha

446 2222

A cross between a gentlemen's club and an English pub, The Old Manor offers firm favourites including shepherd's pie, chicken in a basket and steaks. The cosy little venue is casual and relaxed, with a big-screen TV and comfy chairs. With a great view over the city centre, this is the perfect place to settle down with a pie and a pint. The hotel is on Al Muntazah Street, close to the junction with Wadi Musheireb Street. Map 5 C2

Salsa

Mexican

Marriott Doha

441 1177

Serving favourites such as sizzling fajitas, big steaks and a choice of enchiladas, this lively Mexican restaurant is a great place to come with friends. There are also lighter options of tasty salads on the menu, but portions are generous, and most mains come served with refried beans and Mexican rice. The live band will put everybody in the party mood – and help you dance off your dinner. Map 4 F2

Seasons
Mediterranean
Mövenpick Hotel Doha
429 1111

This restaurant has a variety of theme nights including French, Swiss, Asian and seafood. The Friday brunch is also popular, where kids are not only welcomed, but also supervised and well-entertained. The all-you-can-eat buffet may not be as large as some of the other hotels, but the seafood and sushi are outstanding and the cheese is excellent. The staff are friendly and eager to please, but not overbearing.

Map 5 E2

Taj Rasoi
Indian
Marriott Doha
429 8888

Serving specialities from around India, Taj Rasoi offers diners traditional dishes cooked with great skill. The mouthwatering menu of tandoori, curries and breads will leave guests impressed and full. Many dishes are also prepared at the table. Top picks from the evening menu are available at lunch, and there is plenty of choice for vegetarians.

Map 4 F2

Get Your Pizzeria!

Like most fastfood options in the city, there is no shortage of pizza in Doha. International pizza chains like Pizza Express and Pizza Hut are in the malls and around the rest of the capital. They all offer a takeaway service and most will deliver. Yellow Cab Pizza (488 8310) near TV Roundabout is particularly good, and the pizza stand close to Costa Coffee in Centrepoint Mall offers a nice variety by the slice. The local Italian restaurants will also pack you up a pizza to take home.

Tajine
Souk Waqif

Moroccan
435 5554

Dim light shines out of brass lamps and reflects off ornately carved wood trim, making Tajine a perfect spot for a romantic night out or quiet evening with friends. The menu revolves around the traditional tajine – a covered clay pot used for both cooking and serving. Moroccan food tends to rely on spices, and the resulting flavour is earthy and mellow. None of the dishes are spectacular, but the setting is well worth it. Map 5 C2

The Tent
Al Bustan Hotel

Arabic
432 8888

As soon as you enter, the traditional design of the furniture, the soft lighting, and the aroma of shisha will awaken your senses to this truly Middle Eastern experience. The food is a great example of Arabic cooking, and the waiters are more than happy to help make ordering easier. It's a good spot for a romantic evening or to relax after a long day, but reservations are recommended if you are planning to come after 22:00. Map 5 F2

Thai Noodles
Oppostie Souk Asiery

Far Eastern
443 4220

Tucked away in the heart of the souk area, you might need help finding this little piece of Thailand in Doha – but it's worth the effort. As you enter, you are greeted with big smiles and the aromas of traditional Thai cooking. Open for breakfast, lunch and dinner, the extensive menu offers a huge choice of Thai and oriental dishes. The popularity of this place speaks volumes about the excellent food. Map 5 D2

Bars

Cigar Lounge
Sharq Village & Spa   425 6666

Appropriately dark and stately, this classic cigar lounge appeals
to both the aficionado and the occasional smoker. Choose from
an impressive collection of cigars or select one of the in-house
options, which are rolled on the spot. Don't miss the uniquely
designed ceiling fans that sway gently back and forth. Map 5 E2

Piano Piano
Mövenpick Hotel Doha   429 1111

As the name suggests, entertainment here comes courtesy of
a pianist. Food is available from the Seasons restaurant, but
the setting and atmosphere are probably more conducive
to drinking than eating. Remember this is the old Mövenpick
Hotel, not the new Mövenpick Towers. Map 4 F2

Nightclubs

The Pearl Lounge Club
Marriott Doha   429 8888

This smart club has a reputation for mixing perfect cocktails.
Completely separate from the hotel, it has its own identity,
playing ambient music early evening then switching to a
variety of more upbeat styles. Only members and guests can
come on weekend nights, but on other nights if you look
smart you should be welcome. The dress code is more relaxed
over the summer, but jeans are not allowed for men. Map 4 F2

Entertainment

Qatar's live entertainment scene may be in its infancy, but that doesn't mean there isn't plenty of choice to keep you busy.

Cinemas

Unlike five years ago, today's Doha has plenty of cinemas, and with the opening of the Villaggio cinemas in early 2009, movie-goers have even more choice. Almost all the major releases come out here and they're not far behind the western release dates – but movies with what is considered 'unsuitable' content, such as *Brokeback Mountain*, are banned and some films end up suffering from gratuitous editing. However, gruesome horror pictures are very popular. There is also a big market for Arab and Indian films. English language films aren't dubbed, they just have Arabic subtitles. You can find listings in the local papers.

Comedy

There is only one comedy venue in Qatar, the Ramada Plaza, but amateur theatre group Doha Players (575 5102, www.dohaplayers.com) sometimes holds cabaret nights for its members.

The Laughter Factory
www.thelaughterfactory.com   441 7417
The Laughter Factory, a company that brings in international comedians to tour the Gulf, comes to Doha once a month

for two nights. Three stand-up comics try to avoid the hecklers and get maximum laughs. The standard is usually pretty good, and most of the comics are British (but you get a few other nationalities too). The shows take place in the Shehrazad Bar (p.191) and often sell out, so get your tickets in advance from the hotel. Entry is QR 90, and shows start at 20:00. The bar serves pub food before the acts start and the shows are non-smoking.

Concerts & Live Music

There is no purpose-built concert venue yet, but two concert halls are being constructed at the Cultural Village in West Bay, one of which has been designed especially to host opera and ballet productions. In general, Qatar gets plenty of politicians and business people visiting, but very few entertainers make their way through the country. On occasion, big names do make an

Internet Cafes

Whether you want to get online while enjoying a drink or bite to eat, or you just don't have your own connection at the hotel, there are a few cafes and eateries around town with PCs available for customers to use. Qtel is also increasing its network of wireless Hotspots at hotels, restaurants and coffee shops. These allow users with Wi-Fi enabled devices to access the internet for a small fee. Current locations include the InterContinental Hotel, the Merweb Hotel, both branches of Eli France (Salwa and City Center Doha), La Maison du Café (Salwa and Royal Plaza Mall), Le Notre, Grand Café, Crepaway, Mint Cafe and Fauchon.

appearance – Placido Domingo played at The Pearl in 2008, and Bryan Adams caused much excitement at Al Sadd stadium a few years ago. The big hotels occasionally stage concerts, as does the National Theatre, but marketing can be vague or non-existent and you only find out about the event after it has happened. The annual Dunestock festival showcases local talent in the great outdoors (see p.35 for more information).

Fashion Shows

Qatar is not particularly known for hosting big gala events and shows, but as the country grows and continues to nurture its image as a world-class destination this could well change. There are a couple of fashion shows that are sporadically held during the year by various non-profit organisations such as the American Womens' Association (www.awaqatar.com) and Virginia Commonwealth University's School of Fashion Design (www.qatar.vcu.edu).

Theatre

The best-known theatrical company in Qatar is Doha Players. Made up of talented amateurs and volunteers, the group has been staging English-language productions for over 50 years. It no longer has its own theatre, but the company has raised funds and is now drawing up plans for a new venue. In the meantime, Doha Players has been using various venues around the capital including Garvey's (p.190), Doha Sailing Club and, for bigger productions like the annual pantomime and musicals, the College of the North Atlantic. Check out forthcoming productions on www.dohaplayers.com.

Qatar National Theatre

Profile

208 Culture
214 History
220 Qatar Today

Culture

Numerous international influences combine to create a culture that embraces modernity without shunning tradition.

Modern Qatari culture is an interesting mix of traditional Islamic values and western influence. One of the first things a visitor notices is the Qatari national dress – long, white dishdashas for men and elegant, flowing black abayas for women. The clothing acts as a constant reminder that, although Qatar's developments are propelling it into a globalised future, the country will always hold on to its rich heritage.

Food & Drink

Qatari Cuisine

Spending time in this region is an ideal opportunity to familiarise yourself with pan-Arabic cuisine. Street restaurants selling shawarma, falafel, tabbouleh, hummus and fresh fruit cocktails are a good place to start. Many of the most common Arabic delicacies originated in Lebanon and have been adopted by other parts of the Arab world. That's not to say other Arab countries don't have their own culinary heritage.

The traditional Qatari cuisine is heavily influenced by Indian and Iranian cooking, and its central location exposed it to many spices and ingredients not found in other Arabic cuisines. Early traders introduced new spices and flavours that have become essential in Qatari cooking. Cinnamon, saffron,

Al Wanis Shisha Terrace

turmeric, nuts (especially almonds and pistachios), limes and dried fruits all add interesting flavours to well-known Qatari dishes like ghuzi, harees and machbous.

Arabic Coffee

An important ritual of hospitality, traditional coffee (or gahwa) is mild with a distinctive taste of cardamom and saffron. It is served black without sugar, although dates are presented at the same time to sweeten the palate. It is polite to drink about three of the tiny cups if offered. To refuse the coffee is seen as a refusal of the host's generosity. Shake the cup as a sign that you don't want another refill.

Dietary Restrictions

Pork is not consumed by Muslims, and cannot be bought anywhere in the country. Pork aside, Muslims are forbidden to eat the meat of an animal that has not been slaughtered in accordance with the Islamic code, or halal. Alcohol is also forbidden in Islam and you'll find that the only place for non-Muslims to get a drink is in licensed hotels or sports clubs.

Shisha

Smoking a shisha pipe is an important part of socialising for locals. It is often savoured in cafes while chatting with friends. Shishas are filled with water, and the tobacco, which has a texture similar to molasses, is available in different flavours. Even if you don't smoke cigarettes or cigars, you should try shisha at least once; the smoke is 'smoothed' by the water, creating a much milder effect.

Religion

For Qataris, Islam is more than just a religion, it is a way of life. Qataris are generally conservative and the majority practise their religion. The basis of Islam is that there is only one God (the same God as Christianity and Judaism) and that Prophet Muhammad is the messenger of God. Islam is based on five pillars: profession of faith, praying, fasting, pilgrimage to Mecca in Saudi Arabia, and giving charity. Islam's holy book is the Quran. There are two main forms of Islam: Sunni and Shia. Almost 90% of Qataris are Sunni.

Islam requires believers to pray five times a day. Calls to prayer, which are reminders of the prayer times, are broadcast from loudspeakers installed on the minarets of the many mosques. Praying must be preceded by ritual cleansing, so washing facilities can be found in buildings and public places. Mosques are usually packed with mostly male worshippers on Fridays, when they get to listen to a sermon, or khotbeh, given by a preacher or imam.

Fasting from sun up to sun down is observed for a whole month during Ramadan, which is the ninth month of the Islamic calendar and determined by the moon. Eating in public is prohibited during the day, and most restaurants are closed until sundown, except for some in major hotels. Alcohol is never served or sold during the holy month or on holidays. A religious celebration, Eid Al Fitr, follows the month of fasting. Around 70 days after Eid Al Fitr, Muslims celebrate Eid Al Adha, which translates as the festivity of sacrifice, in which Muslims slaughter sheep and distribute part of the meat to the poor.

Politics

Qatar is governed by hereditary rule. The current head of state, His Highness Sheikh Hamad bin Khalifa Al Thani, has introduced many reforms and steered the country towards a more open and democratic system of government. The Emir's brother, Sheikh Abdullah bin Khalifa Al Thani, is the prime minister, and the Emir's son, Sheikh Tamim bin Hamad Al Thani, is the crown prince and heir apparent.

The Emir holds legislative and executive powers and he appoints a Council of Ministers by an emiri decree. The role of the Council of Ministers is threefold: to draft, discuss and vote on proposed laws after consultation with the Advisory (or Consultative) Council; to approve the national budget; and to monitor the performance of ministers.

A 2003 referendum saw a permanent constitution overwhelmingly approved by the local people. The constitution promises freedom and equality, and provides for a 45 member Advisory Council, two thirds of which are elected by the public, with the remaining members appointed by the Emir. The first council elections were held in 2007.

Qatar held historic democratic elections in 1999 (subsequently held every four years) for the Central Municipal Council (CMC), made up of 29 councillors representing the country's municipalities. Women were eligible to vote and stand for election, and in 2003, Sheikha Al Jefairia was the first woman to be elected, and received a record highest number of votes in the 2007 election. The CMC has consultative (but no executive) powers and is aimed at improving services in the municipalities.

Going to prayer at a local mosque

History

From its early ties to the expansion of Islam to its more recent oil-fuelled development, Qatar's history is surprisingly rich.

Archaeologists have uncovered evidence of human habitation in Qatar possibly dating back to the fourth and fifth millennia BC. In the fifth century BC the Greek historian Herodotus referred to the ancient Canaanites as the original inhabitants of Qatar. The country features on old maps of the region, suggesting that Qatar was known to seafarers and traders of the time.

After Islam swept the region in the seventh century AD, Qatar's history was forever linked to the religion. The inhabitants of Qatar are said to have aided the formation of the first Islamic naval fleet. The country also became well known for the quality of its textile manufacturing (especially cloaks) and for the making of arrow heads.

Around the 13th and 14th centuries, Qatar enjoyed a favourable relationship with the Caliphates (successors of the Prophet Muhammad) in Baghdad and it became an important centre for pearl trading. Evidence from this Abbasid era (Caliphate rule) can be seen in the architecture of Murwab Fort on Qatar's west coast. In the 16th and 17th centuries the Portuguese were a powerful force throughout the Gulf region. To protect itself from occupation and aggression, Qatar aligned with the Turks. This saw the start of over three centuries of rule by the Ottoman Empire, although throughout this period the real power in Qatar remained with local sheikhs.

The ancestors of today's ruling family, the Al Thanis, arrived in Qatar in the early 18th century. Originating from a branch of the Bani Tamin tribe from Najd in modern-day Saudi Arabia, they first settled in southern Qatar before moving to the north of the peninsula in the mid 1700s. Qatar, and especially the northern town of Zubara, continued to be a key centre for the pearl trade.

Dawn Of Doha

In the mid 19th century, Sheikh Mohammed bin Thani established Al Bidda, the modern city of Doha, as the capital and seat of power. Soon after, in 1868, a treaty negotiated with the British recognised him as the first official Emir of Qatar. This treaty signed with the British also recognised Qatar's independence. Three years later, Sheikh Mohammed signed another treaty with the Turks, accepting protection against external attack. A Turkish garrison was established in Doha, but the relationship was an uneasy one and the Ottomans were forced to abandon Doha in 1915. In 1916, Sheikh Abdullah Al Thani signed a further treaty with the British promising not to enter into relations with any other power without prior consent. In return, Britain guaranteed the protection of Qatar 'from all aggression by sea'.

A number of factors, including worldwide economic depression and the introduction of cultured Japanese pearls, led to an almost complete collapse of the Gulf's pearling industry in the 1930s. Pearling had been the mainstay of Qatar's economy for generations, and while life for the country's inhabitants had never been easy, this development was a desperate blow. The region was plunged into dire poverty, and disease was rife among the undernourished people.

In the midst of despair there was hope though. Bahrain had become the first Gulf state to discover oil earlier in the decade and, in 1935, Sheikh Abdullah signed the first Oil Concession Agreement with the Anglo-Persian Oil Company. Drilling began and oil was discovered in Dukhan in 1939. The onset of the second world war halted production almost immediately, and the first oil wasn't exported from Qatar until 10 years later. This new-found wealth transformed the lives of the population beyond recognition, as the rulers set about modernising the country's infrastructure and creating healthcare and education facilities. The wealth generated from oil exports, and the discovery and exploitation of the world's largest single reservoir of natural gas, means that Qatar today enjoys one of the highest levels of income per capita in the world.

Independence

In 1968, Britain announced its intention to withdraw from the Gulf region. Qatar entered into talks with Bahrain and the Trucial States (now the United Arab Emirates) with the intention of forming a federation, but agreement could not be reached and after Bahrain withdrew from the discussions, Qatar followed suit. When the British left in September 1971, Qatar became officially independent. The ruler then was

Traditional fort in Al Wakra

Sheikh Ahmed bin Ali Al Thani, but he was succeeded the following year by his cousin Khalifa bin Hamad Al Thani, with the full support of the ruling family, the Qatari people and the armed forces. Sheikh Khalifa led Qatar into a period of continued prosperity, especially thanks to the huge rises in oil and gas prices during the 1970s. He also went some way to diversifying Qatar's economy by establishing facilities for producing goods such as steel and fertiliser.

In June 1995, Sheikh Khalifa was succeeded as Emir by his son and heir, the Crown Prince and Minister of Defence, Sheikh Hamad bin Khalifa Al Thani. Sheikh Hamad continued with the modernisation and liberalisation programmes he had started as Crown Prince. Press freedom was extended and, in 1997, the state-funded satellite TV news channel Al Jazeera was launched, quickly gaining a reputation for its outspoken coverage of sensitive topics. In 1999, the country took its first steps towards democracy, when free elections for the Central Municipal Council were held. Women were allowed to stand for office as well as vote. Sheikh Hamad is seen as a progressive ruler and is widely respected by Qatar's citizens, who benefit from the country's wealth in the form of free or subsidised healthcare, education and housing.

More recently, Qatar has established itself as a centre of regional diplomacy. In 2008, Sheikh Khalifa and his aides brokered a power-sharing deal between the disparate political parties of Lebanon. The feat was hailed by the international community for its difficulty. Qatar has also used its diplomatic savvy to speak with leaders from Syria, Iran, Palestine and even Israel.

Qatar Timeline

7th century AD	Islam sweeps the Arabian peninsula. Inhabitants of Qatar help form the first naval fleet
13th century	Qatar becomes established as a key pearling centre
16th century	Qatar aligns with the Ottomans as protection against the Portuguese
Early 18th century	Ancestors of the Al Thani arrive in Qatar
Mid 18th century	Mohammed Al Thani establishes Al Bidda (Doha) as capital
1868	Treaty signed with the British, recognising Qatar's independence, and Mohammed Al Thani as the first Emir
1871	Treaty signed with the Turks, accepting protection against external attack
1915	The Ottomans abandon Doha
1916	A further protection treaty signed with the British
1930s	Pearl industry collapses
1939	Oil found in Dukhan
1949	First oil exported from Qatar
1971	Discovery of the world's largest single concentration of natural gas
1971	Qatar declares independence on 3 September
1995	Sheikh Hamad Al Thani succeeds his father Sheikh Khalifa as Emir of Qatar
2006	The 15th Asian Games are held in Doha

Qatar Today

With more than enough natural resources to rely on, Qatar has focused its future on arts and culture instead of glitz and glam.

People & Economy

Fifty years ago, this tiny Gulf peninsula was only beginning to blossom – oil had just begun to be exported, and the region-leading healthcare and education projects that define the country were only in the planning stages. The Qatar of today may still rely on oil to fuel its growing economy, but its physical landscape is hardly recognisable. Much of the infrastructure started back then has been completed and a drive along the plush roads witnesses towering skyscrapers where palms trees and beach huts once stood.

The makeup of Qatar's inhabitants has changed as well. Thanks to booming industry and favourable business conditions, the country has been flooded with expatriate workers. Today, only around 20% of the 930,000 people living in Qatar are Qatari, the rest hail from south Asia, Iran, other Arab countries, and Europe.

Thanks mainly to its abundant reserves of oil and gas, Qatar has one of the strongest and fastest-growing economies in the world. Analysts predict that in the near future, the country's gross domestic product (GDP) per capita will overtake that of Switzerland, effectively making Qatar the richest nation on earth.

Qatari Nationals on the Corniche

Qatar's GDP for 2007 was over QR 240 billion, nearly a 25% increase on the previous year, and the IMF has forecast an average annual GDP growth of 11% a year until 2012. The oil and gas sector accounted for 73% of the GDP in the first half of 2008.

Proven oil reserves currently stand at 15 billion barrels. However, in order to become less reliant on oil and diversify the economy to some degree, Qatar is investing heavily in its liquefied natural gas (LNG) industry. The country's natural gas reserves stand at 910 trillion cubic feet, ranking Qatar third in the world behind Russia and Iran. The state-owned Qatargas has been ramping up its production and hopes to be the world's largest exporter of LNG by 2012.

Tourism

In contrast to its Gulf neighbours, Qatar doesn't necessarily want to attract mass tourism. Instead, it aims to attract high-income sectors such as cultural and educational tourism and the Mice market (meetings, incentives, conferences and exhibitions). To help achieve this the government is investing a massive $15 billion to develop Qatar's infrastructure, including a new airport to cater to the growing number of tourists. In 2006, approximately 730,000 people visited the country but this figure is estimated to climb to 1.4 million a year by 2010.

While most of the major international hotel chains are already represented in Qatar, the investment in infrastructure will see a host of new hotels and resorts emerge to cater for the anticipated growth in visitor numbers. At present, 41 new hotels are under construction, and by summer 2010, Qatar will have an estimated 10,000 hotel rooms. As well as stand-alone hotels, there are a number of projects currently under way that will include facilities for tourists, such as the Lusail development, the Al Fareej Resort, Entertainment City, and, of course, The Pearl Qatar.

In a further boost for the tourism sector, the 2006 Asian Games was a huge success and helped put the country on the map as a leading host of sporting events in the region – Qatar has been selected to host the fourth Indoor Asian Games in 2011. The influx of tourism prompted by such events has led to a number of multi-million dollar projects that will bring Doha's infrastructure up to premium international standards.

New Developments

Education City   www.qf.edu.qa

Developed by the Qatar Foundation, Education City is
already home to a number of institutions and international
university campuses. Projects currently at the planning stage
or under construction include a 350 bed teaching hospital,
a convention centre, and the Qatar Science and Technology
Park. Upon completion, the site will house 30 buildings,
including a museum and sports facilities.

Lusail   www.lusail.com

This mixed-use development will eventually cover 35 square
kilometres and be able to accommodate around 200,000
people. Occupying a strip of coastline 15km north of Doha,
the project will have 10 districts featuring marinas, hotels,
entertainment and leisure, office towers, lots of shopping, two
golf courses, and various types of housing. With an estimated
$5 billion price tag, it is scheduled for completion by 2010.

New Doha
International Airport   www.ndiaproject.com

Construction is well under way on Doha's new airport, located
a few kilometres east of the existing airport and partly on
reclaimed land. Designed to cater to the growing number of
visitors expected over the coming years, the airport will be
built in three phases. When complete, in 2015, the airport will
be equipped to handle 50 million passengers a year. The new
airport will serve as a global hub for Qatar Airways.

Oil & Gas

www.qp.com.qa

Qatar Petroleum is investing billions of dollars in the country's oil and gas facilities and infrastructure. Projects include the expansion and upgrading of facilities at Dukhan City (Qatar's first oil centre), Mesaieed Industrial City, and Halul Island. Ras Laffan Industrial City is already the world's largest liquefied natural gas export facility, and a new $1.6 billion plant will soon process gas to be pumped over 370km through a dedicated pipeline being laid between Qatar and Abu Dhabi.

The Pearl Qatar

www.thepearlqatar.com

Perhaps the best known of Qatar's current development projects, The Pearl is a new island complex built on reclaimed land off the shore of the West Bay Lagoon. It will feature apartments, town houses and villas, plus retail outlets, restaurants, entertainment venues, and three five-star hotels. It was the first development in Qatar to offer freehold property to non-locals. The cost of the project is around $2.5 billion, and the first villas were handed over at the end of 2008.

Qatar-Bahrain Causeway

The 'Friendship Causeway' will be a 40km road link between Qatar and Bahrain. Some people view it as an extension of the King Fahd Causeway that connects Bahrain to Saudi Arabia, meaning that when complete it will be the longest fixed link in the world. The project will take up to five years to complete, and could cost as much as $4.7 billion.

Modern Doha

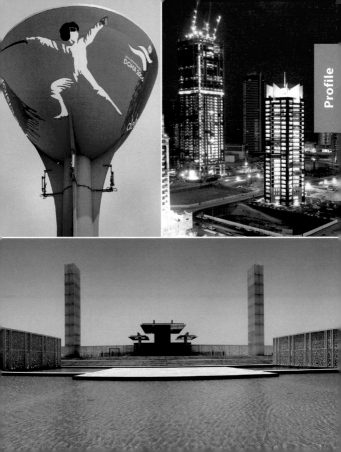

Maps

228 Doha Overview
230 Legend & Street Index
232 North Doha
234 Diplomatic Area
236 South Doha
238 Souk Area &
Doha Corniche

226

Map 1

Doha Overview

N

AL KHEESA

AL KHARAITIYAT

QATAR UNIVERSITY

WEST BAY LAGOON

AL DUHAIL NORTH

AL ZAGHWA

AL DUHAIL SOUTH

NEW DISTRICT OF DOHA 67

AL ZAGHWA

AL GHARRAFA

MADINAT KHALIFA (NORTH)

AL MARKHIYA

AL ZAGHWA

NEW DISTRICT OF DOHA 64

KHALIFA ST

MADINAT KHALIFA (SOUTH)

EDUCATION CITY

AL RAYYAN AL QADEEM

KULAIB

WADI AL ASAIL (WEST)

AL WAJBAH

AL LUQTA

WADI AL SAIL (WEST) BIN OMRAN

AL MESSILA

AL HITMI AL JADEED

AL RAYYAN AL JADEED

AL AMIR

AL RAYYAN RD

MURAYKH

AL SADD

AL MIRQAB AL JADEED

IBN MAHMOOD SOUTH

MUAITHER NORTH

AL SOUDAN NORTH

AL NASR

AL AZIZIYAH

AL SOUDAN SOUTH

AL ASIRI

MUAITHER SOUTH

AL WAAB

SALWA RD

AL MAAMOURA

AL KULAIFATAL JADEEDA

AL AZIZIYAH

AL MURRAH

SALWA ROAD SOUTH

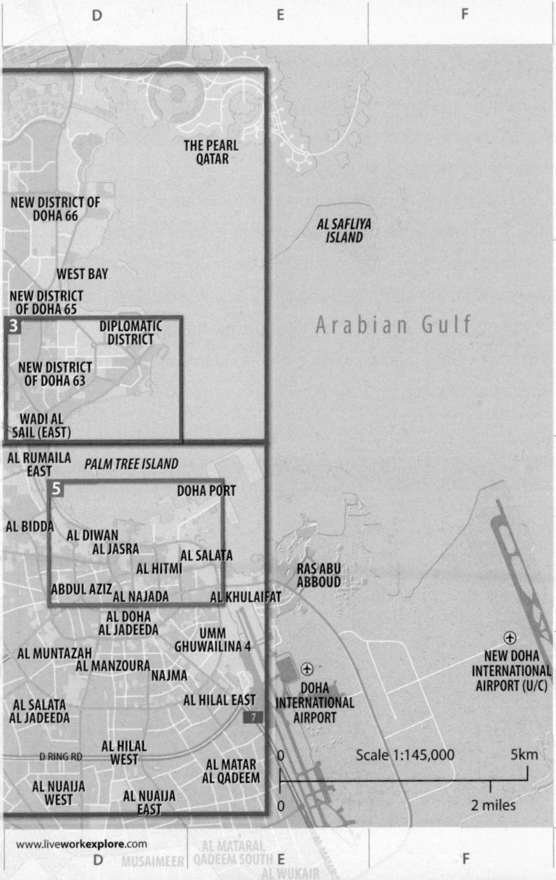

Map 1

D E F

N

1

THE PEARL
QATAR

NEW DISTRICT OF
DOHA 66

AL SAFLIYA
ISLAND

WEST BAY

NEW DISTRICT
OF DOHA 65

3

DIPLOMATIC
DISTRICT

2

Arabian Gulf

NEW DISTRICT
OF DOHA 63

WADI AL
SAIL (EAST)

AL RUMAILA
EAST

PALM TREE ISLAND

5

DOHA PORT

AL BIDDA

AL DIWAN
AL JASRA

AL SALATA

3

AL HITMI

ABDUL AZIZ AL NAJADA

AL KHULAIFAT

RAS ABU
ABBOUD

AL DOHA
AL JADEEDA

UMM
GHUWAILINA 4

AL MUNTAZAH

AL MANZOURA

NAJMA

NEW DOHA
INTERNATIONAL
AIRPORT (U/C)

AL SALATA
AL JADEEDA

AL HILAL EAST

7

DOHA
INTERNATIONAL
AIRPORT

4

D RING RD

AL HILAL
WEST

Scale 1:145,000   5km

AL NUAIJA
WEST

AL NUAIJA
EAST

AL MATAR
AL QADEEM

0

2 miles

© Explorer Group Ltd. 2009

AL MATARAL
QADEEM SOUTH

MUSAIMEER

AL WUKAIR

Legend

The following maps cover most of Doha, and the inside back cover contains a country map of Qatar. The most important malls, museums, hotels and parks are marked on the map.

You may also have noticed the large pull-out map at the back of the book. This is intended to give you an overview of the city. The perforated edges mean you can detach it from the main book, so you have even less to carry. Or, if you and a travel companion have different plans for the day, you can take one each – so if one of you wants to soak up the culture, while the other wants to shop, there's no need for compromise.

Legend

H	Hotel		Land		Highway
🏛	Heritage/Museum		Pedestrian Area		Major Road
✚	Hospital		Built up Area/Building		Secondary Road
	Park/Garden		Industrial Area		Other Road
	Agriculture		Cemetery	⊐==⊏	Tunnel
	Shopping	★	Visitor Attraction	E	Embassy
	Education	$	Bank	𝒊	Tourist Info
	Stadium	Theatre R/A	Junction Name	✈	Airport
⛽	Petrol Station	AL BIDDA	Area Name	⚑	Golf Course
				✉	Post Office

Street Names	Map Ref	Street Names	Map Ref
22 February St	4-B1	Al Sadd St	4-C2
Abu Hamour St	4-C4	Al Shamal Rd	2-B4
Ahmed Bin Mohammed Bin Thani St	5-C4	Al Shedaida St	4-B1
Al Amir St	4-C3	Al Waab St	4-B3
Al Asmakh St	5-C3	Al Wahda St	2-D3
Al Bidda St	5-B1	Ali Bin Abdullah St	5-D2
Al Bustan St	4-B3	Ali Bin Abi Thalib St	4-D3
Al Corniche St	5-E2	Ambassadors St	3-D1
Al Diwan St	5-B3	Arab League St	2-B2
Al Funduq St	3-E3	B Ring Rd	5-D4
Al Gharrafa St	2-A3	C Ring Rd	4-E3
Al Haloul St	4-B4	C Ring Rd (Suhaim Bin Hamad St)	4-D2
Al Istiqlal St	3-B2	D Ring Rd	4-D3
Al Ittihad St	2-A3	Diplomatic St	3-D1
Al Jamiaa St	2-C2	E Ring Rd	4-D4
Al Jazira Al Arabiya St	4-B1	Grand Hamad St	5-D2
Al Khafji St	2-B2	Huwar St	2-A4
Al Khufoos St	4-A2	Jabr Bin Mohd St	5-D2
Al Luqta St	2-A4	Jasim Bin Hamad St	4-C2
Al Maadeed St	4-D4	Khalifa St	2-C4
Al Markhiya St	2-B3	Majlis Al Taawon St	3-C3
Al Maszhabiliya St	2-A3	Makkah St	2-B4
Al Matar St	4-F3	Najma St	4-E3
Al Meena St	5-E3	Omar Bin Al Khattab St	2-B4
Al Muntazah St	4-E4	Onaiza St	2-D2
Al Muthaf St	5-E2	Ras Abu Abboud St	5-E3
Al Rayyan Al Qadeem St	4-A1	Salwa Rd	4-B4
Al Rayyan Palace St	4-B2	Sports City	4-A3
Al Rayyan Rd	5-A2	Wadi Musheireb St	5-B3
Al Reday St	4-B1	West Bay Lagoon St	2-D2
Al Rumeilah St	5-A1	Wholesale Market St	4-D4

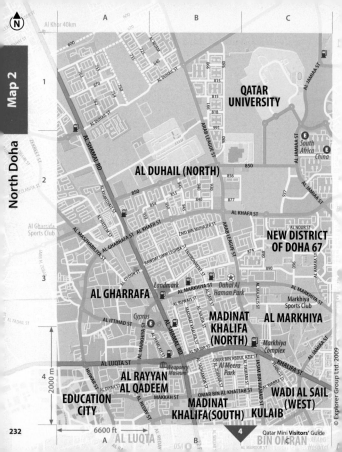

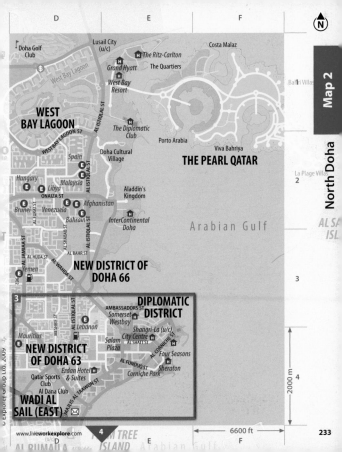

Map 2

North Doha

N

D E F

Doha Golf
Club

Lusail City
(u/c)

The Ritz-Carlton

Costa Malaz

Grand Hyatt

The Quartiers

Bahri Villas

West Bay
Resort

WEST
BAY LAGOON

West Bay Lagoon

WEST BAY LAGOON ST

AL ISTIQLAL ST

The Diplomatic
Club

Porto Arabia

Viva Bahriya

Doha Cultural
Village

THE PEARL QATAR

La Plage Villas

2

Spain

Hungary

Malaysia

Libya

ONAIZA ST

Aladdin's
Kingdom

Brunei

Venezuela

Afghanistan

AL LUQTA ST

Bahrain ST

InterContinental
Doha

Arabian Gulf

AL SA
ISL

AL SHABAB ST

AL ISTIQLAL ST

AL BAHR ST

AL JAMIAA ST

AL HUDA ST

AL WAHDA ST

NEW DISTRICT OF
DOHA 66

3

Yemen

3

DIPLOMATIC
DISTRICT

AMBASSADORS ST

Somerset
Westbay

AL ISTIQLAL ST

MESHIREB ST

Lebanon

Shangri-La (u/c)

City Centre

Mauritius

Salam
Plaza

AL SHATT ST

NEW DISTRICT
OF DOHA 63

AL CORNICHE ST

Four Seasons

Sheraton

Ezdan Hotel
& Suites

AL FUNDUQ ST

Qatar Sports
Club

Corniche Park

MAJLIS AL TAAWON ST

Al Dana Club

WADI AL
SAIL (EAST)

4

2000 m

© Explorer Group Ltd. 2009

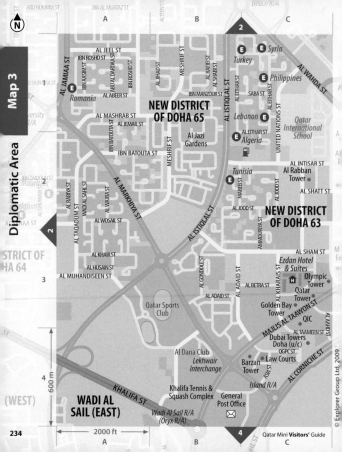

Map 3

N

Diplomatic Area

ABU HURAIRA ST

IBN AL MUATAZ ST

BEACH R/A

2

A B C

AL AITEN ST

AL JEEL ST

IBN AL ROSHD ST

IBN AL DARDAA ST

IBN QASSIM ST

Romania

AL ABEER ST

AL JAMIAA ST

AL JIHAD ST

MESHRIF ST

AL BAFEF ST

AL SHABI ST

IBN MANZOUR ST

AL ISTIQLAL ST

AL EITHAR ST

Turkey

E

E

Syria

AL WAHDA ST

E

Philippines

SABA ST

AL EITHAR ST

AL MASHRAB ST

AL JEMAIL ST

NEW DISTRICT OF DOHA 65

E

Lebanon

AL EITHAR ST

UNITED NATIONS ST

Qatar International School

IBN BATOUTA ST

IBN BATOUTA ST

MESHRIF ST

Al Jazi Gardens

ALEITHAR ST

E

Algeria

University R/A

1

ABU HURAIRA ST

IBN ZAIDOUN ST

Mauritania R/A

2

AL MURQAB ST

Belgium R/A

2

AL RABYA ST

AL TAQADUM ST

WADI AL SAHL ST

AL WAJBA ST

AL WOSAIL ST

AL MARKHIYA ST

AL ISTIQLAL ST

Tunisia

E

MARJEH ST

Al Rabban Tower

AL INTISAR ST

AL JOOD ST

AL SHATT ST

AL JOOD ST

AMMOURIYA ST

NEW DISTRICT OF DOHA 63

DISTRICT OF DOHA 64

AL KHAIR ST

AL HUSAIN ST

AL MUHANDISEEN ST

AL CONDOLES ST

AL ADAID ST

AL ADAID ST

AL BETRA ST

AL SHAM ST

Ezdan Hotel & Suites

AL KHARAIS ST

Qatar Sports Club

3

Olympic Tower

Qatar Tower

Golden Bay Tower

QIC

MAJLIS AL TAAWON ST

AL TAAMEEN ST

Dubai Towers Doha (u/c)

QGPF CST

AL KHAISI ST

Al Dana Club

Lekhwair Interchange

Barzan Tower

ASPI ST

Law Courts

AL CORNICHE ST

Island R/A

4

600 m

WADI AL SAIL (EAST)

KHALIFA ST

Khalifa Tennis & Squash Complex

General Post Office

Wadi Al Sail R/A (Oryx R/A)

(WEST)

WEST

© Explorer Group Ltd, 2009

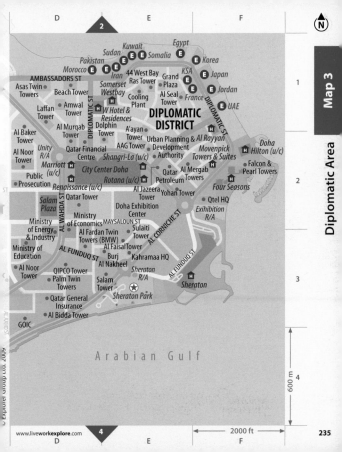

Map 3

Diplomatic Area

Map 4

South Doha

Qatar Mini **Visitors'** Guide

© Explorer Group Ltd. 2009

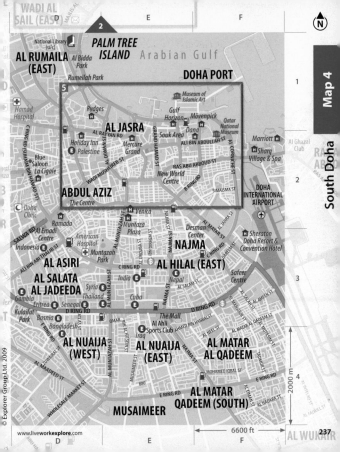

Map 5

(N) N

A   **B**   **C**

Rumeilah Park

URBDS T

AL RUMEILAH ST

MAJLIS AL TAAWON ST

AL AQSA ST

AL AQSA ST

Ministry of Interior

AL DAKHLIYA ST

AL BIDDA ST

Arabian Gulf

AL CORNICHE ST

Dhow Harbour

1

AL BIDDA

AL QURTUBI ST

AL KHANDAQ ST

Rydges

QNA

ABU FIRAS ST

AL BIDDA ST

AL DIWAN

Emiri Diwan

Corniche R/A

Grand Mosque

AL ASMAKH ST

AL JASRA

Souk Waqif

ABU HANEEFA ST

FASS ST

AL BIDDA ST

Clock Tower

Souk Jaidah

AL RAYYAN RD

Holiday Inn

OMAR AL MUKHTAR ST

AL FAISAL ST

AL FIRDOUS ST

AL DHAHIYA ST

AL FAYHAA ST

PALESTINE ST

Gulf Plaza

Mercure Grand

UKAZ ST

Al Qal'a ST

AL SOUK ST

AL KOT ST

2

Palestine

AL DIWAN ST

UKAZ ST

ABDULLA BIN THANI ST

AL DAHNAA ST

Al Koot Fort

Regency

MUSHEIRIB

AL FIRDOUS ST

AL KAHRABAA ST

15 YARDS ST

ALITTEHAD ST

AL DEERA ST

AL MIRQAY ST

AL BID ST

AL NAJADA ST

AL ASMAKH ST

Doha Palace

AL BUSAYYIR ST

AL GHADEER ST

AL NAKHEEL ST

WADI MUSHEIREB ST

MASAR ST

UMM WSHAH ST

3

AL QUMRI ST

AL KHALEEJ ST

AL AHMADI ST

AL MAZROUA ST

AL ADHWAA ST

UMM WSHAD ST

UMM WSHAD ST

AL JASSASIYA ST

AL MAYMOUN ST

IBN HANBAL ST

AL AREEQ ST

BARZAN ST

AL NUHA ST

IBN AL ATHEER ST

WADI MUSHEIREB ST

ABDUL AZIZ

AHMED BIN MOHAMMED BIN THANI ST

IBN MAHMOUD ST

IBN AL JAROOD ST

IBN GHROUT ST

Jaidah Flyover

AL ZUBARA ST

AL YAQAMEEN ST

IBN AL HAITHAM ST

AL SALAMI ST

AL SHERMAN ST

AL FARABI ST

AL SUWAIDI ST

AL DOHA ST

AL JADEEDA ST

IBN AL AWWAM ST

AL KHATRAB ST

4

SALWA RD

ABU ABBAD ST

IBN AL ARQAM ST

B RING RD

Apollo Clinic

The Centre

238

600 m

2000 ft

Qatar Mini **Visitors'** Guide

© Explorer Group Ltd. 2009

Map 5

N

D · E · F

Qatar Flour Mills

DOHA PORT

Museum of Islamic Art

Al Bandar

Customs & Port Authority

Customs R/A

Gulf Horizon

AL CORNICHE ST

Al Hitmi Complex

Museum Park

QCB

Qatar Islamic Cultural Centre

ABDULLAH BIN JASSIM ST

AL BALADIYA ST

Youth & Sports Authority

Mövenpick

Salata Park

Qatar National Museum

Museum R/A

Souk Feleh

Souk Nasr

Souk Al Aseiry

Souk Al Dira

Souk Al Jabor

AL SAFLIYA ST

AL MAHRA ST

AL SALATA

Dana

Al Bustan

Ras Al Nassa Restaurant

Ras Al Nassa

AL AHMED ST

AL AALIYA ST

AL AALIYA ST

AL MUTHAF ST

Al Jaber Group

AL LOULOU ST

AL CORNICHE ST

ALI BIN ABDULLAH ST

RAS ASHAIRIJ ST

AL HITMI

BAKIR AL AQRB ST

AL BESHARWA ST

SHERAOUH ST

AL MAARIF ST

AL ASHAT ST

Al Fardan Centre

AL MEENA ST

YAFA ST

Ras Abu Aboud R/A

GRAND HAMAD ST

AL MUDAF ST

AL DOSTOUR ST

VW R/A

IBN AL JAWZI ST

C RING RD

AL NAJADA

AL MAHAR ST

DAR AL KUTUB ST (Sana R/A)

Sana Fashion

IBN ZUHAIR ST

RAS ABU ABBOUD ST

Giant Stores

AL SALMI ST

ABU BAKR AL SIDDIQ ST

SALWA ST

Woqod HQ

New World Centre

IBN ABDUL MUTTALIB ST

BAIT AL HIKMA ST

AL WIFAQ ST

SAEED BIN AL AAS ST

A AHMAD ST

KHABAR ST

QURAISH ST

AL IBREEZ ST

Al Watan Centre

La Rose De Sable Apts

B RING RD

IBN KHALDOUN ST

BABIL ST

AL KHUWAIR ST

SIMAISMA ST

AL MATAR ST

Capital Security Dept

SIMAISMA ST

AL MIQDAD ST

AL FUSTAT ST

AL FATEH ST

SALAH AL DEEN ST

HIDRAMOUT ST

AL WAAB ST

AL ROSE ST

SHERAM ST

UMM GHUWAILINA ST

AL AMAN ST

AL JAHRA ST

B RING RD

IBN KHALDOUN

600 m

Index

A

AAB Rent-A-Car Company	41
Active Qatar	98
Admiral's Club	170
Adrenaline Junkies	16
Afternoon Tea	165
Air France	19
Air India	19
Airlines	19
Al-Muntazah	49
Aladdin's Kingdom	58
Al Aziziyah	178
Albatross	194
Al Bidda Park	66
Alcohol	148
Al Dana	194
Alfardan Automobiles	41
Al Hamra	156
Al Hubara	164
Al Jassasiyeh	86
Al Khaima	156
Al Khor Museum	87
Al Koot Fort	80
All'Aperto	195
Al Liwan	194
Al Luqta Street	70, 176
Al Majlis	156
Al Mirqab Street	126
Al Muftah Rent a Car	41
Al Muntazah Park	74
Al Rakiyat Fort	87
Al Rayyan Road	54, 154
Al Rumeilah Park	15
Al Sadd	54, 154
Al Sadd Street	54, 126
Al Samakh	135

Al Sayyad	165
Al Shaheen	165
Al Shaqab Stud	70
Al Sulaiman Rent a Car	41
Al Wajbah Fort	54
Al Zubara Fort	88
Al Zubara Town	88
Anglo-Persian Oil Company	216
Animal Souk	74
Annual Events	34
Applebee's	181
Arabian Adventures	94
Arabic Coffee	210
Around Souk Waqif	130
Asha's	182
Asia Live!	195
Aspire Academy	75, 112
Aspire Park	75
Aspire Tower	75
Assaha Lebanese Cultural Village	195
Aussie Legends	174
Automatic	157
Avis	41

B

Balhambar	173
Bar Directory	153
Bargaining	128
Basic Arabic	25
Beauty Centre & Spa	120
Beijing	182
Beirut	173
Bentley's Grill	182
Best Of Qatar	16
Bicycle	38

Big Spenders	16	Chopsticks	157	Dine On A Dhow	11
Biman Bangladesh	19	Ciao	184	Diplomacy	218
Bio-Bil Health	120	Cigar Lounge	201	Diplomatic Area	58, 162
Black Pearl	95	Cinemas	202	Diplomatic	
Blogs	31	Cinnzeo	163	Club	106, 107, 110, 111
Blokart Paradise	108	City Center Doha	134	Diving	102
Blue Salon	138	City Tours	93	Doha	48
Boat	39	Climate	22	Doha Corniche	64, 172
Boat Tours	92	CloudNYN	161	Doha Cultural Festival	35
Bombay Balti	183	Coffea	155	Doha Fort (Al Koot Fort)	80
Books	31	Coffee	210	Doha Golf Club	103, 116
Brasserie On The Beach	166	Comedy	202	Doha International Airport	18
Bridal Souk	132	Concerts	203	Doha Players	204
British Airways	19	Convention Hotel	106	Doha Sub Aqua Club	102
Brunch	181	Corniche	196	Doha Summer Festival	36
Bubbles	190	Costa Coffee	164	Doha Zoo	76
Budget Car & Van Rental	41	Council of Ministers	212	Door Policy	147
Bukhara	177	Country Tours	94	Dos & Don'ts	22
Bus	39	Crepaway	184	Dress Code	28
Button and Bow Souk	132	Crime	22	Drink Driving	191
		Culture	208	Drinking	148, 208
C		Culture Buffs	17	Driving	39
Cafe Batteel	183	Cup & Cino Coffee House	155	Dune Bashing	12
Café Plus	179	Customs	19	Dunestock	35
Caffe Amici	163	Cycling	114		
Camel Racing	114	Cyprus Airways	19	**E**	
Camel Rides	100			Eating Out	147
Camping	100	**D**		Economy	220
Campsites	49	Dahal Al Hamam Park	70	Education City	71, 223
Car Hire	39	Dawn Of Doha	215	Egypt Air	19
Carpets	140	Delta Airlines	19	Eid	211
Car Rental Agencies	41	Department Stores	138	Eid Al Adha	36
Central Market	127	Developments	223	Eid Al Fitr	36
Centrepoint	135	Dhow	11	Electricity	23
Chili's	183	Dhow Charters	101	Eli France	180
Chingari	184	Dietary Restrictions	210	Elite Limo	41

Emir 212
Emirates 19
Entertainment 202
Equestrian Sports 115
Essentials 2
Europcar 41
Exploring 50
Ezdan Hotel & Suites 45

F

Fahd Bin Ali Palace 55
Fashion Shows 204
Fauchon 185
Female Visitors 23
Fishing 103
Fish Market 76, 166
Food 208
Football 115
Four Seasons Hotel 45
Friday Market 129
Friendship Causeway 224
From The Airport 18
Fuddruckers 177
Fun City 55
Further Reading 30

G

Garvey's 190
Gas 224
Getting Around 38
Getting There 18
Going Out 144
Gold Souk 130
Golf 103, 116
Gondolania 76
Grand Gourmet 157

Gulf Adventures 95, 110
Gulf Air 19
Gulf Paradise 49

H

Habanos 170
Halal 210
Health Spas 120
Hertz Rent A Car 41
Highland 138
History 214
Horse Riding 104
Hotel Apartments 49
Hotspots 126
Hyatt Plaza 136

I

Il Rustico 173
Il Teatro 166
IM Pei 64
Independence 216
INet Café 58
InterContinental Doha 45
Internet 27
Internet Cafes 203
Irish Harp 169
Islam 211
Islamic Art 10
Islamic Art, Museum Of 64
Islamic New Year 37

J

Jewellery 140
JG Sandwich Cellar 193
Johnny Rockets 185
Jungle Zone 77

K

Kayaking 104
Kebab King 196
Khalifa International Stadium 75
Khalifa Street 70, 176
Khor Al Adaid 90
Kitesurfing 106
KLM 19
Kuwait Airways 19

L

La Cigale 46
La Cremiera 193
La Dolce Vita! 164
La Mer 167
Landmark Shopping Mall 134
Language 24
Laughter Factory 202
La Villa 198
Layali Lounge 186
Layali Restaurant 186
Le Central 158
Le Cigalon 158
Le Monot 186
Le Pain Quotidien 180
Lina's 180
Live Music 203
Local Cuisine 148
Local Knowledge 22
Losail 116
Lusail 223

M

Madison Piano Bar 161
Magazines 30
Main Tour Operators 94

Mannai Autorent	41
Maps	31
Markets	128
Marks & Spencer	138
Marriott Doha	48
Maxim	187
Media	30
Merch	139
Ministers, Council of	212
Mint Living Cafe & Restaurant	187
Money	24
Mosques	93
Motorbike Racing	36
Motorsports	116
Muhammad, Prophet	214
Muntazah Park, Al	74
Museum Of Islamic Art	10, 64
Museum Park	66
Musheirib	126
Music	203

N

National Car Rental	41
National Day	37
National Museum	66
Natural gas	221
Neo	187
New Developments	223
New Doha International Airport	223
Newspapers	30
Nightclub Directory	153

O

Oil & Gas	224
Old Souk	128

Omani Market	129
Orientalist Museum	82
Oryx Farm	90

P

Pakistan International Air	19
Palm Tree Island Boat Company	101
Paloma	167
Parasailing	106
Paul	181
Pearl Qatar, The	60, 224
Pearl Divers	102
People	220
People With Disabilities	25
Piano Piano	201
Pizza	199
Places Of Worship	93
Places To Stay	44
Plaza Hotel	49
Police	27
Politics	212
Ponderosa	188
Population	220
Porcini	168
Pork	210
Powerboating	107
Powerboat Racing	35, 118
Prestige Rent a Car	41
Profile	206
Prophet Muhammad	214
Public Holidays	32

Q

Q-Dive Marine Center	102, 109
Qatar-Bahrain Causeway	224

Qatar Airways	19
Qatar Checklist	6
Qatar Classic Squash Championship	118
Qatar ExxonMobil Open	119
Qatargas	221
Qatari Cuisine	208
Qatar International Adventures	95
Qatar International Rally	117
Qatar International Tennis Tournaments	34
Qatar International Tours	95, 100, 103, 109, 110
Qatar Kite Surfing Club	106
Qatar Marine Sports Federation (QMSF)	118
Qatar Masters Golf Tournament	34
Qatar Motor & Motorcycle Federation	117
Qatar National Heritage Library	77
Qatar National Museum	64, 66
Qatar Racing & Equestrian Club	104, 115
Qatar Sailing & Rowing Federation	107
Qatar Timeline	219
Qatar Today	220
Quad Bikes	107
Qube	191

R

Radio	30
Ramadan	211

Ramada Plaza Doha 46
Ras Al Nasaa 174
Ras Laffan Industrial City 224
Ray's Reef 55
Rayyan Road 54
Regatta Sailing Academy 93, 108
Religion 211
Restaurant Directory 150
Retaj Residence 49
Richoux 168
Ritz-Carlton Doha 120
Royal Jordanian 19
Royal Plaza 137
Royal Wings 49
Ruby Wu's 188
Rumeilah Park (Al Bidda Park) 66

S

Safari Tours 94
Safety 22
Sahara Hotel 49
Sailing 107
Sakura 188
Salam Plaza 139
Salsa 198
Salwa Road 126, 178
Sand Boarding 108
Saudi Arabian Airlines 19
Sealine Beach
  Resort 47, 100, 104, 107
Seasons 199
Sharq Village & Spa 47
Shehrazad Lounge
  Bar & Terrace 191
Sheikh Faisal Bin Qassim
  Al Thani Museum 13, 71

Sheraton Doha
  Hotel & Resort 47, 106
Sheraton Gardens 60
Sheraton Park Cafe 172
Shisha 210
Shisha Cafes 149
Shop In Style 6
Shopping 122
Shopping In Qatar 124
Shopping Malls 134
Shops Outside Doha 125
Sightseeing 92
Six Senses Spa at Sharq
  Village & Spa 121
Sixt Rent A Car 41
Sky View 161
Snap Up Fresh Fish 9
Snorkelling 109
Somerset West Bay 48, 49
Souk Al Ahmed 132
Souk Al Asiery 132
Souk Al Dira 132
Souk Al Jabor 132
Souk Area 80, 192
Souk Haraj 133
Souk Nasser Bin Saif 133
Souks 128
Souk Waqif 14, 80, 130, 192
Souvenirs 141
Spa & Wellness Centre 121
Spas 120
Spectator Sports 112
Spikes Lounge 169
Squash 118
SriLankan Airlines 19

Star of India 158
Step Back In Time 8

T

Tailoring 142
Tajine 200
Taj Rasoi 199
Tangia 160
Taxi 40
Telephone 27
Television 30
Tennis 119
Textiles 142
TGI Friday's 177
Thai Noodles 200
Thai Snacks 160
Theatre 204
The Bay Club 101
The Corniche 7
The Garden 196
The Inland Sea (Khor Al Adaid) 90
The Italian Job 185
The Lagoon 167
The Laughter Factory 202
The Library 190
The Library Bar &
  Cigar Lounge 170
The Mall 137
The Old Manor 198
THE One 176
The Pearl Lounge Club 201
The Pearl Qatar 60, 224
The Ritz-Carlton Doha 46
The Spa 120
The Tent 200
The Third Line 82

Thursday Market	129
Time	28
Timeline	219
Tipping	28
Tourism	222
Tour Of Qatar	34
Tours	92
Trucial States	216

U

Umm Salal Mohammed Fort	90

V

Vegetarian Food	149
Venue Directory	150
Villaggio Mall	135
Visas	19
Visiting Qatar	18
Visitor Information In Qatar	20

W

W Hotel & Residences	48
Wadi & Dune Bashing	109
Wajbah Fort, Al	54
Wakeboarding	110
Walking	42
Waqif Arts Center	82
Watches	140
Water	23
Water Babies	17
Waterskiing	111
Websites	31
West Bay	58, 162
Windtower House	83
Winter Wonderland	58
Wok Mee	168

Y

Yen Sushi Bar	160

Z

Za Moda	169
Zero Tolerance	191
Zubara, Al	88

Explorer
Products

Residents' Guides

All you need
to know about
living, working
and enjoying life
in these exciting
destinations

Abu Dhabi Amsterdam Bahrain Barcelona
Beijing Berlin Dubai Dublin
Geneva Hong Kong Kuala Lumpur Kuwait
London Los Angeles New York New Zealand
Oman Paris Qatar Shanghai
Singapore Sydney Tokyo Vancouver

Mini Visitors' Guides

Perfect pocket-sized visitors' guides

Activity Guides

Drive, trek, dive and
swim... life will never be
boring again

Check out www.liveworkexplore.com

Mini Maps

Fit the city in your pocket

Maps

Wherever you are, never get lost again

Photography Books

Beautiful cities caught through the lens

Lifestyle Products & Calendars

The perfect accessories for a buzzing lifestyle

Check out www.liveworkexplore.com

Explorer Team

Publishing

Publisher Alistair MacKenzie
Associate Publisher Claire England
Assistant to Associate Publisher
Kathryn Calderon

Editorial

Group Editor Jane Roberts
Lead Editors Tim Binks, Tom Jordan
Online Editor Helen Spearman
Deputy Editors Jake Marsico,
Pamela Afram, Siobhan Campbell
Senior Editorial Assistant Mimi Stankova
Editorial Assistants Grace Carnay,
Ingrid Cupido

Design

Creative Director Pete Maloney
Art Director Ieyad Charaf
Account Manager
Christopher Goldstraw
Junior Designer Jessie Perera, Didith Hapiz
Layout Manager Jayde Fernandes
Designers Mansoor Ahmed Kalathingal,
Rafi VP, Shawn Zuzarte
Cartography Manager
Zainudheen Madathil
Cartographers Juby Jose,
Noushad Madathil, Sunita Lakhiani
Traffic Manager Maricar Ong
Traffic Coordinator Amapola Castillo

Photography

Photography Manager Pamela Grist
Photographer Victor Romero
Image Editor Henry Hilos

Digital Solutions

Digital Solutions Manager
Derrick Pereira

Senior IT Administrator R. Ajay
Senior Software Engineer
Bahrudeen Abdul Kareem
Web Developer Anas Abdul Latheef

Sales & Marketing

Media Sales Area Managers
Laura Zuffa, Paul Santer,
Pouneh Hafizi, Stephen Jones
International Media Sales Manager
Peter Saxby
New Business Development Manager
Ben Merrett
Corporate Sales Area Manager
Hannah Brisby
Sales & Marketing Coordinator
Lennie Mangalino
Marketing Manager Kate Fox
Marketing Executive Annabel Clough
Marketing Assistant Shedan Ebona
International Retail Sales Manager
Ivan Rodrigues
Retail Sales Coordinators
Sobia Gulzad, Michelle Mascarenhas
Retail Sales Supervisor Mathew Samuel
Retail Sales Merchandisers
Johny Mathew, Shan Kumar
Senior Retail Sales Merchandisers
Ahmed Mainodin, Firos Khan
Warehouse Assistants
Ashfaq Ahmad Thachankunnan,
Mohamed Riyas Chakkiyath
Drivers Najumudeen K.I., Shabsir Madathil

Finance & Administration

Finance Manager Michael Samuel
Office Manager Shyrell Tamayo
Junior Accountant Cherry Enriquez
Public Relations Officer Rafi Jamal

www.liveworkexplore.com

Contact Us

▶ **Reader Response**
Post your comments and suggestions on our discussion boards,
or fill out our reader response form online.
Log onto **www.liveworkexplore.com**

▶ **Newsletter**
If you would like to receive the Explorer newsletter packed with
special offers, latest books updates and community news please
send an email to **marketing@explorerpublishing.com**

▶ **General Enquiries**
We'd love to hear your thoughts and answer any questions
you have about this book or any other Explorer product.
Contact us at **info@explorerpublishing.com**

▶ **Careers**
If you fancy yourself as an Explorer, send your CV (stating the
position you're interested in) to **jobs@explorerpublishing.com**

▶ **Designlab and Contract Publishing**
For enquiries about Explorer's Contract Publishing arm and
design services contact **designlab@explorerpublishing.com**

▶ **Maps**
For cartography enquries, including orders and comments,
contact **maps@explorerpublishing.com**

▶ **Corporate Sales**
For bulk sales and customisation options, for this book or any
Explorer product, contact **sales@explorerpublishing.com**